NEW FRONTIERS IN MISSION

NEW FRONTIERS
IN MISSION

Edited by
PATRICK SOOKHDEO

Exeter, U.K.
THE PATERNOSTER PRESS

BAKER BOOK HOUSE
Grand Rapids, U.S.A.

CONTENTS

76748

Preface

Wheaton '83 was an international evangelical conference on 'The Nature and Mission of the Church'. It was convened by the World Evangelical Fellowship and co-sponsored by a number of churches and Christian organizations from around the world. Under the general theme, three separate consultations took place of which the second consultation focused on 'The Nature and Mission of the Church in New Frontier Mission'. The Strategy Working Group of the Lausanne Committee for World Evangelization, the Missions Commission of the World Evangelical Fellowship, Partnership in Mission and the Catalyst Committee of Edinburgh '80 cooperated together to provide joint leadership for this event.

The 140 carefully selected and invited participants represented mission societies from the Western as well as the Two Thirds World, churches and para-church agencies, theologians as well as practitioners, and those involved in education and church planting from a variety of backgrounds. In the pre-conference study process, during which papers were prepared and circulated, as well as during the two-week consultation, the 140 participants grappled with the following issues: to define the unfinished frontier task and to direct the attention of the Church to the task of world evangelization: to state clearly which groups need to be reached with the Gospel and identify the resources for carrying this out, with particular attention to equipping mission agencies from the Two Thirds World, as well as mobilizing them and providing them with the history and experience of the Church worldwide in the task of world evangelization; to gain a commitment to action, so that existing missions and emerging mission agencies will work together in reaching the unreached and meet together to coordinate the different ministries, thereby making valuable new associations with both thinkers and doers; to alert the churches in internal and external perils which obstruct effective missionary enterprise, and to identify resources and training facilities in responding to the unfinished task; and finally to plan for the follow-on in responsible

1

Non-Western Missions:
The Great New Fact of our Time

PAUL PIERSON

1. INTRODUCTION

In 1942, Archbishop Temple of Canterbury called attention to 'the great new fact of our time', the existence of the Christian Church, for the first time in history, in virtually every nation on earth. In many countries, the Church was weak, constituting only a tiny part of the population; nevertheless, it was there. Although the goal of the Student Volunteer Movement, the 'evangelization of the world in this generation', had not been reached, the 'great new fact' highlighted by Temple was still a magnificent and significant milestone in redemptive history.

However, I suggest that the subject of this essay constitutes an even more important development. The great new fact of our time, forty years after Temple's statement, is *the rapid growth of the non-Western Christian missionary movement*. None of us can foresee all of its implications for both Church and world, but they will go far beyond anything we can foresee in their positive effect on the history of the Church. Never in history has any message been communicated by so many people of such a variety of races, languages, cultures and nationalities as is the case with the Gospel today. And the corollary is that never before has any message been heard (and in many cases joyfully received) by men and women of so many races, cultures and nationalities. There is still much to be done, but a quantum leap has been made toward the fulfilment of the promise made to Abraham, that through his seed, all the families on earth would be blessed (Gen. 12:3).

The non-Western Protestant missionary movement is not completely new. We must remember magnificent groups like the

The sheer number of men and women of non-Western churches who may be called to cross cultural evangelism adds to this potential. When the entire Church (North American, South American, Asian, African and European) is seen as the sending and support base for mission, world evangelization will take a significant new step forward. We may be sure that God will lead his Church to create new and in many cases less cumbersome mission structures through our Asian, African and South American brethren. In looking at a very institutionalized church in Thailand in 1980, I gained the distinct impression that, just as that country had become Buddhist through monks who lived their simple lifestyle among the rural people, it would not become significantly Christian until followers of Christ began to demonstrate a simple Christian lifestyle at the village level.

Secondly, this movement will serve as *a healthy corrective to the perception in many parts of the world that Christianity is a Western religion*, inseparably bound up with Western culture. In many cases this has led to agonizing dilemmas for some who, drawn to Christ, believed that in order to be his disciples they had to reject their own cultural heritage. Remembering McLuhan's phrase, 'The medium is the message', we are reminded that before Paul and Silas crossed over from Asia Minor into Europe to proclaim the good news of the God who accepted people of every race and culture on the basis of faith alone, they were led to add two others to their team of Hellenistic Jewish believers. One was Timothy, who was half Greek; the other was Luke, who apparently was fully Greek. An excellent parallel is seen in organizations which bring black and white to proclaim the Gospel together in Southern Africa today. The multi-national, multi-racial missionary movement, with various groups working in cooperation and mutual affirmation, can witness powerfully to the Gospel by demonstrating something sadly lacking in our modern world, a model which affirms the validity of cultural diversity and an overarching unity in Christ at the same time.

Thirdly, I believe this new development will lead each participating body into a *deeper and more biblical understanding of the Church*. We all seem to suffer from a deep-seated tendency to focus in upon ourselves, our own church, culture and nation. Yet the constant tug of the Holy Spirit, clearly seen in Acts and elsewhere, is to turn our attention toward the other, the stranger, the one beyond our gates. I can still remember hearing John of its hearers as it so often came with the imposition of Western power and culture.

Obviously, Western missionaries cannot deny their own identities and the cultures from which they come, even though they must make a much greater effort than heretofore to distinguish between the Gospel and their culture. But the non-Western movement, with most of its missionaries coming from nations which are not perceived as powerful on the world scene, may make it easier for its recipients to hear the biblical message of a Servant Lord who calls his followers to become a Servant People. The self-emptying aspect of the Christian life might again be restored to its rightful prominence, and replace the competitive individualism so characteristic of Western culture and much of Western Christianity. Perhaps when the power of Western technology and culture is less obvious, the power of the Gospel will be seen more clearly.

3. LESSONS FROM THE HISTORY OF WESTERN MISSIONS

However, for all the positive implications of the non-Western missionary movement, there are also a number of dangers to be avoided. There are lessons, positive and negative, to be learned from the history of Western missions, of which I want to focus on a few on the most important.

First, it is probable that cases will occur in which Western churches and societies should share resources with non-Western mission structures. In these situations a high degree of trust and openness must be developed to ensure the authenticity and independence of the non-Western agency. In the years following World War II, a small and precarious — but effective — mission of Brazilian Presbyterians to Portugal was destroyed by well-meaning North American boards who 'helped' too much with personnel and funds. On the other hand, the Friends Missionary Prayer Band in India once turned down the offer of a large infusion of American funds in order to maintain itself as a completely Indian mission. Between the extremes indicated by those two examples there will be situations which call for cooperation, but Westerners must follow the lead of their brethren of other cultures to avoid the dangers of smothering nascent movements, on the one hand, and excessive aloofness on the other.

Secondly, the question of missionary selection and preparation

a. PIPKA is to determine what personnel are to be recruited and accepted;
b. The partnership is subject to constant evaluation by all concerned.
c. PIPKA is responsible for running a missionary training programme for candidates (be they Indonesian or foreigners).

Fourthly, it is important to remember that it is never enough merely to send out missionaries and then forget about them. Spiritual and material support are needed if the mission is not to find itself with a large drop-out rate and little effectiveness. Along with this it is important to realize that careful research and periodic evaluation are not incompatible with trust in the Holy Spirit.

In the fifth place the newer missions should strive to maintain their mobility, flexibility and focus. No mission structure is immune to the dangers of institutionalization and absorption into the concerns of the churches which it has established. To relate positively to the local churches without becoming focused exclusively on them and forgetting the unreached—this will not be the problem of Western missions alone.

Finally, there is the need for frequent consultation. God has much to teach us through our brothers and sisters of other churches and cultures. The value of the encouragement and mutual stimulus to greater faithfulness can scarcely be overestimated.

NOTES

(1) Charles Cristiano, 'PIPKA, An Indonesian Response to Mission', *International Bulletin* Vol. 6 No. 4, Oct. 1982

passed; but these have produced very little practical result. Colonialism is over. A new day is dawning. Some missionary societies, in particular the denominational ones, have given to their churches the right of self-determination. But many others still have a long way to go. The mentality of colonialism can still live on. Many churches recognise their great indebtedness to the Western missionary movement, knowing that in a very real way they owe their existence to the costly sacrifice of many missionaries on their behalf, but it is the same spirit of sacrifice that is now being called for, on the part of the Western missionary movement. Can she break the cycle of dependence which now exists, so that the church worldwide can enter an era of true interdependence? Can she free herself from the shackles of her historic past with its mistakes and wrong attitudes and face the future in successfully ushering in a new age of mission?

There is a real sense of frustration in some sections of the church overseas, as they wait for this to happen. In the second Quito consultation of 1978 the Bolivian group issued the following statement:

> We have come to this meeting with the desire to approach some problems of a neurotic nature in the Lord's work in our continent, and to seek, together with the representatives of foreign mission present here, solutions for those problems. However, after two days of discussion, we are under the impression that this objective isn't being reached. Because of this, we would like to pose the following questions and inquietudes, in hope that they will serve as a channel for the deliberations of the final day of this consultation.
>
> 1. We question whether, up to now, there has been true dialogue between the Latin Americans and the representatives of foreign missions. We feel that there has been only monologue on the part of the Latin Americans. In view of this, we ask: Have the mission representatives really listened? Have they understood us? Have they accepted what we've said up until now? We would like a reaction to these questions.
> 2. We would like the missionary personnel too, with complete honesty, objectivity and frankness, to make a self-examination of their structures, organizations and methods of work, and the difficulties that many of them have in their relationships with the national church. We also recognise the necessity to analyse the limitations and difficulties that in the same sense, the national staff and organisations can have.
> 3. We ask for a concrete reaction concerning a model of inter-

It went on to suggest to Western missions the following:

- To urge the churches of like Biblical faith and para-church organisations to cooperate with one another in order to fulfill their tasks more effectively.
- To encourage both Asian and Western missionary societies to cooperate with one another in missionary associations and training programmes and put an end to divisions which have little relevance in Asia.
- To urge Asian and Western missions not to start new counterparts of their denominations, but rather to work together with existing churches of like faith without multiplying new structures.
- To request that the founding missions should facilitate and encourage churches to unite with similar bodies of like faith.
- To call upon para-church organisations, especially international ones, to act always in the best interests of the national church and not to lure away gifted personnel by offering them far more generous remuneration than the church can afford.
- To urge missionary societies to avoid the paternalism that delays unnecessarily the handing over of leadership to national Christians.
- To request Asian and Western missions not to maintain indirect control of national churches through financial strings.
- The Lausanne Congress of 1974 cast new light on this need for continued involvement. It recognised that 'a reduction of foreign missionaries may sometimes be necessary to facilitate the national church's growth in self-reliance and to release resources for unevangelised areas.'

Not all would accept this principle of reduction. Dr Tokunboh Adeyemo, General Secretary of AEAM, sees the decline of missionary personnel in Africa as adding to the problems of the church there. He remarks, 'Nationals have been called upon to shoulder responsibilities for which they have had little or no preparation. Some of the ministries that flourished under mission administration have been closed up since the national church took over, partly because of lack of trained personnel and partly because of lack of interest on the part of the nationals, or all of these combined.'

Some would argue that this is not necessarily a bad thing and see it as breaking the cycle of dependence. 'The church in Africa,' claims John Mbiti, 'has been very missionary minded but only in terms of receiving missionaries and depending on them.' But whatever the differences of emphasis between the various thinkers, the main lesson remains clear: Western missions need to examine the existing undergraduate seminaries. Nor does the answer lie in sending Africans to Western countries for post-graduate training. Both these courses will be necessary for some years to come but they are inadequate and increasingly suspect by African communities who see the church yielding to excessive Western influence. We are grateful for this necessary interim help, but the time is overdue to replace it with our own African Answer.' (This quotation comes from a brochure for a new Nairobi School of Theology.)

3. DESIRE FOR FINANCIAL INDEPENDENCY

At a recent consultation between church and mission leaders in Tanzania the continued financial support of the church by the mission was discussed. Three distinct positions were taken up.

There were those church leaders, a minority, who argued for total cessation of funds coming from outside. They felt that the receiving of funds from the West was compromising their position in the eyes of their fellow countrymen and that it continued to breed dependency on their part. This initial breaking of financial links would also extend to other areas of dependence and would last until the church achieved full self-reliance and self-sufficiency.

Second, there were those church leaders, the majority, who argued for a continuation of the existing situation and saw the relationship between church and mission as presenting no problem.

Finally, there were those who argued that it would not be right to engage in a total break of fellowship as this would be unjustifiable in the light of Scripture, yet that at the same time there was a need to achieve self-sufficiency. They suggested that this would best be approached over a period of time, as church and mission worked together towards this end.

Younger nationals are increasingly conscious of the stigma of financial dependency. They point to those of their leaders who are spending their time jet-setting to various conferences across the world; to others who have an increased standard of living and possess Western luxury items because of their links with a mission; to the privileged few who go off to further study at Western colleges; and so on. They also note that because the mission has the money it is able to influence, if not control, decisions affecting the church, such as the appointing of leaders, the setting up of special the money it is able to influence, if not control decisions include theological emphases.

5. THE DESIRE FOR SOCIAL JUSTICE

Christians in societies that are politically, socially and economically deprived are increasingly aware of the relevance of the Gospel to these areas of life. Some see missions as agents of change and so call upon mission societies to educate their home constituency about situations of deprivation. Rene Padilla expressed it thus: 'How can rich Christians be united in mission as long as many of them (especially in the West) adopt an ostentatious life-style while the large majority of them (especially in the underdeveloped world) are unable to satisfy essential human needs? The poverty of the Third World places a question mark over the life-style of people, and particularly of Christians in the West.'

Ronald Sider adds, 'If a mere fraction of North American and European Christians should begin to apply Biblical principles on economic sharing among the worldwide people of God, the world would be utterly astounded.'

Others see a need for missionaries and societies, wherever possible, to become involved in human rights issues. An example is Bishop Wickremesinghe, Bishop of Kurunagala, Sri Lanka, who delivered the 1979 annual sermon of the Church Missionary Society. In it he declared, 'In the era of imperial expansion the Church saw politics in the context of evangelism and mission. Christians in church and nation at that time were catalysts of change, agents of a new order of life. As a contemporary Asian Christian I see evangelism and mission in the context of politics.' He went on to urge missionary societies to 'foster and send some missionaries . . . to function as community agitators, where political conditions permit expatriates to do so.'

Not all Two Thirds World church leaders would agree with either or both of these positions. Many would err on the pietistic side and see involvement in politics and in economic issues as an involvement in the 'world'. They therefore shy away from this area.

CONCLUSION

The desire of most churches in the non-Western world is for a true partnership. They would like missionary agencies to act with

Integration

PETRUS OCTAVIANUS

PREFACE

Before discussing integration in detail, we need to consider three fundamental issues in introducing the subject:

1. *Political Background*

In these last forty or so years since World War II, about 100 Asian and African nations have gained independence. ˙

Looking at it from the psychological angle, it is evident that they will want to express their capacity to stand on their own feet. That in itself is something positive. But the way of expressing it may look negative, in that it comes out in explosions and eruptions. In the course of the gaining of independence the governments often took over churches or church institutions, stressing that leadership must be handed from the missionary to the national worker. A transitional period is a period of crisis. The important thing is bound to be that we do our best to minimize these crises.

In the relationship of integregation the cross of Christ has a place to operate.

2. *Historical Background of Missions*

At present, the Second World is still playing the most important role in missions (mission statistics in 1978 show that from a total of 55,930 missionaries in the world, 50,200 (88.3%) come from the First and Second World, while 5,730 or 10.1% come from the Third World).

It is clear that the understanding of international missions in

THREE FORMS OF COOPERATION

Within the development of missions we meet three main forms of cooperation between the foreign missions and the national groups:

- a) *Partnership.* This is the most common and widely practiced form.
- b) *Workers on Loan* for a limited time and for a specific task.
- c) *Integration.*

It is necessary to have a genuine appreciation of all the different forms, and at the same time obediently to embrace and enter into the specific form which the Lord gives to a particular mission.

In the mission the present writer belongs to, we hold to integregation as the God-given line for us. The members of our fellowship come from very different backgrounds nationally and denominationally. If we start to separate ourselves according to our differences and emphasize our individual uniqueness rather than seeing the whole, then we are surely in for difficulties. We have to place unity first. This has to be our fundamental principle. Thus we have to hold to one particular line, being conscious of the fact that it is not the only way or the best way which would allow us to reject every other way but that it is the way given to us by the Lord. For us this is important not only in relation to the members who come from abroad, but also in relation to the Indonesians among themselves.

The people from Minahasa are quite different from the Javanese, and the Batak from the Timorese, and they all have their own identity, thinking and cultural background. And so we all need to be convinced that the principle of *integration* is the form which God gave to the Indonesian Missionary Fellowship and at the same time remain appreciative of other forms.

A. *Partnership*

Partnership means that two agencies work together, but each runs its own business without interfering with the others.

1. Integration means that we do not hold on to defend ourselves and our interests in relation to others. This has to be applied very widely within an evangelistic fellowship. Everyone has his own identity relating to doctrine and denominational background, level of education and social status. Yet integration dictates that he must not hold on to himself and his identity, for the sake of developing and promoting his ministry together in fellowship with the brethren.

2. Integration means that we seek to identify ourselves with those to whom we minister (cf. John 1:14). This identification is one of the conditions for effective communication between the one who ministers and the one being ministered to. And it is just as important in relationships between evangelistic groups.

3. Integration means that the common needs, the common fellowship and the common ministry are more important than the individual interests of each member.

THE MEANING OF THE WORD 'INTEGRATION'

It is illuminating to look at the actual meaning of the word 'integration'. Webster's dictionary gives the meaning as follows: 'to put or bring together parts into a whole, unify', where the important aspect is that 'unity is in the whole'. The word 'integration' originates from the Latin word *integratus*, which has three main meanings:

  a) 'to make whole or complete by adding or bringing together parts'. The whole consists of the parts, 'yet the whole is different from the parts'.
  b) 'to put or bring parts together into a whole, to make unity.'
  c) In connection with psychoanalysis integration means 'to organise various traits or tendences into one harmonious personality'.

From this we see that the main points is 'the whole, the unity' where the parts have a vital function and develop towards perfection within the whole. With this background of understanding, I want to mention eight aspects of integration in order to clarify what it means in the life of a mission; and I want to state again that it is necessary that each of these aspects be accepted *wholeheartedly* by *every member* of a mission that holds to the line of integration.

outworking of this is surely difficult, because every one of us has to be open and willing to receive help from another. Within the IMF we do not seek to disregard the culturally based 'pluses' which are present, but we do accept that the Lord wants to form us and shape us, and sometimes this happens in a hurting kind of process; and we are convinced that the Lord wants to give us lines of conduct which are commonly acceptable. Therefore, we cannot afford to think that we have individual freedom just to act as we are accustomed, without regard to the habit of others in that same matter.

3. *The educational aspect.*
Within a fellowship the differences in educational background create difficulties. In our mission there are those who have received advanced theological training, there are those who have received education of an intermediate level, and also those who do not have full theological education. And within the IMF every member receives the same financial allowance without regard to the individual's educational standard. This can create tensions and divisions within a fellowship. But the principle of integration helps us to overcome those problems. We recognize that educational prowess can be a 'plus', but the uniting element for us is the fact that we are together in a service and ministry.

4. *The cooperational aspect.*
In selecting leaders we do not favour any particular national background, or social or educational background, but the decisive factor is the proven ability and gift of the individual concerned. Of course, this cannot be separated completely from the educational factor. It is not inevitable that the foreign worker has to be in the lead. If there is an Indonesian capable of exercising leadership, why should there be a foreigner in that place? On the other hand, if the foreigner is able to lead, why should he be rejected? We shall discuss the question of leadership in more detail later, but here we have to hold on to the principle that in working together we do not pay heed to national, educational and other differences. We regard, appreciate, and give place to every member equally in accordance with the ability and gift proven.

5. *The aspect of ministering together.*
We have experienced something very beautiful in working together

within a mission needs our careful consideration because of two things: first, in regard to the future leadership; secondly, because of the development of regional leadership in the ever-widening sphere of the IMF. The increasing number of full members also demands wise leadership in the allocation of places and tasks. (At present we have 180 members, including 135 national workers and 39 foreign workers.) Therefore I want to state three basic conditions for a leader of the IMF. He must be:

a. Spiritually qualified.
b. With an understanding of missions and churches in Indonesia and the world, especially those who enter into a relationship of cooperation with us.
c. Able to function at a national level. This means that he must be recognized by the government and by the churches as a leader.

Of course there are other qualities desirable in a leader, but the three abovementioned conditions are the main ones. Besides that, the leader has to commit himself very definitely to the spiritual principles which have played the decisive role in the development of a mission. In the case of our mission, these principles are: fellowship, faith and holiness. Let us never exchange these spiritual principles and pillars for more human endeavour and efforts.

We have to pray for those who will carry on the tasks within a mission and for its leadership. For this we very much need Indonesian brethren. This is inevitable because of our situation and its history. The political conditions and the signs of the time demand that there be a leadership consisting of Indonesian brethren. This does not mean that we refuse the leadership of non-Indonesians, but it does mean that we have to give attention to the need for strong motivation to be given to the Indonesian brethren who will carry on the leadership. On the other hand, our brethren from outside have to be able to accept and appreciate the leadership exercised by the Indonesian brethren. The principle of integration can ensure a harmonious relationship here. Therefore we look at integration as including the question of leadership.

7. *The financial aspect*

In Acts 4:33-35 we notice two things. First, that the believers brought the money gained through selling their property and laid it at the feet of the apostles. Secondly, that money was distributed a time of adjustment together with the newly applying members from inside the country, in that they live together and learn together the language, the fellowship regulations and culture. In this way the missionary can experience the most natural initial adjustment to the culture and make himself familiar with the constitutional foundation of the country and the overall situation of the churches. He can then develop a sensitivity, appreciation and understanding of the situation in the country and the existing church life. This probationary period lasts for two years, and decides whether the new worker can be accepted into the fellowship.

Integration is only one possible method of working in mission. But I am convinced it can have an application and can serve in solving tensions existent in inter-mission relationships and cooperation in this present century.

The mission structure, therefore, must innovate continuously according to the degree of church growth and her spiritual maturity on mission fields.

A planting structure is not suitable for cultivating time. A cultivating structure has to be renovated to meet the needs for growing time as a third stage. And a growing structure to bring toward maturity has to be reshuffled to become reciprocal in the face of new missions emerging from the former mission field itself.

Western mission seems to have no choice but to engage itself in formation of the fourth stage in cooperation with Two Thirds World mission which has now reached full growth, having passed through the planting, cultivating, and growing stages. The national personnel resources on the fields are gradually becoming weightier than missionary personnel in terms of quantity and quality, educational level, expertise and spiritual ability.

When a national church has turned out to be larger than the supporting mission agencies which have come to that land in its service, there is a dynamic imbalance. And there can be a functional discord between Western missionaries and national leaders over matters which, if left to the decision of the national task force, would have been handled in a much different way.

The purpose of mission is that an established national church is to be not only self-governing, self-supporting, and self-propagating, but also outreaching across its national barriers. Yet the tremendous human and material resource which has been developed by the Western missions for these past 150 years has not yet been mobilized or organized for reaching the unreached frontiers.

The structural inversion and functional discord between mission agencies and national churches could well be solved through united efforts to develop national churches into sending structures.

B. The subordinate relationship of sender and receiver should end

There is no subordinate relation between sender and receiver in the Acts of the Apostles. Paul, the apostle who himself had been sent by another church, took the very churches that received the gospel from him and turned them into sending national organizations within a short span of ten years. The multi-nationalization of the missionary enterprise by Paul avoided the harmful effect which might have been caused by a subordinate pattern and a possible domination by mission bodies.

out world mission simply because they have dispatched a medical doctor, nurse or technician to a hospital established by Westerners, and because they have filled in positions once occupied by Western personnel and now vacant, due to the anti-Western sentiment in these nations.

3. Some Two Thirds World leaders try to justify a claim of 'sending missionaries' because they exchange professors or students with other Two Thirds World countries.

4. Some Two Thirds World missions have sent out one or two missionary families at random to this place and that without doing any reliable research as to the responsiveness of the field, or stating clearly the goals for which they plan to work. Thus they spend much money yet harvest no tangible fruits.

5. Unfortunately it is also true that among the Two Thirds World missionaries some are going around from country to country, after having worked in one mission field just three or four years at most.

6. In the last ten years some promising and potent Two Thirds World leaders have been recruited by strong and capable Western mission agencies, which were thus able to buy out such extraordinary leadership ability as may be found only once or twice in a generation.

7. This situation is quite detrimental to the development of Two Thirds World leadership. Many young Two Thirds World leaders have remained in the West after their studies in the Western countries, with the result that Asian leadership has been curtailed and has withered because of the brain drain.

B. **Emergence of a Two Thirds World competitive elite, and controlled liaison.**

The Two Thirds World church leadership which has prevailed until recently is gradually being replaced in this decade by a group of innovating, enterprising leaders. The latter are by no means routineers, adminstrative liaison officers, or controlled agents.

Their attitude toward the changing world is clear cut; they are afraid of no unknown future, nor of untried projects; they possess

CROSS FERTILIZATION STRUCTURE CONCEPT.

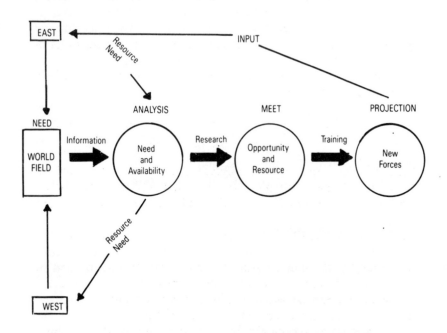

III. HOW TO SHARE THE FUND RECIPROCALLY

Organization, personnel and finance are the three pillars of missionary structure. These three always interact. If however, harmony and effective adjustment among them are not successfully worked out, the innovating tendency will wither away and role regression show forth. For instance, the mutual relationship between Western financial assistance and Two Thirds World mission should not be in the form of so-called 'assistance' but 'East-West joint investment' to a third mission field or project, as in the case of the early apostolic church, in which the churches both of Macedonia and of Corinth had shared in contributions to the impoverished Jerusalem church. Whatever the case, receivers have no choice but to look up to givers and (like it or not) to become West-controlled agents; and role regression reappears.

While stimulated by outside elements, the actual practice is done for and within their own countries.

E. The 'Cross-Border' Approach.

This is made possible only when Two Thirds World missions have grown into maturity in terms of personnel and finances, and come on an equal footing with the Western counterpart in all ways; and when personnel, financial, and technical exchange can be made on a completely equal basis.

IV. HOW TO FORM RECIPROCAL FRONT-LINE RELATIONSHIPS

The arrangements necessary can be divided into *operational* structures and *associative* structures.

A. Operational structures

This signifies a *direct and mutual relation* in missionary operation in the one nation or same region. This is the relation between *activities* and *agents*, between identical activities done by different agents and similar agents carrying out different activities. This may be further divided into *reciprocal* structure and *cooperative* structure.

1. *Reciprocal structures*

This can be divided into *phase one* and *phase two*:

i) Phase one relates itself to what is called 'home' church by Two Thirds World missions, and 'field' church by Western missions.

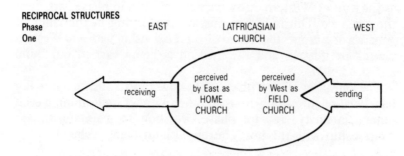

2. Cooperative structures

This can also be divided into two phases:

i) Phase one is in the first place a cooperative structure between two agencies: a Western mission which has pioneered a field in a Two Thirds World country, and another mission from the Two Thirds World which has come to the same field; and in the second place it is a *further* relationship between the latter and its predecessor, the Western mission or field force.

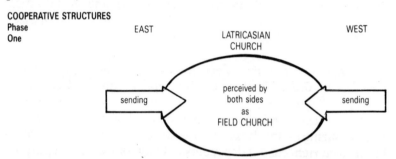

COOPERATIVE STRUCTURES
Phase One

EAST

LATRICASIAN CHURCH

WEST

sending

perceived by both sides as FIELD CHURCH

sending

ii) The case of phase two is rarely seen at this present time, but it will keep on increasing in years to come. It concerns a cooperative structure between churches that are established by Two Thirds World missions and the missions themselves.

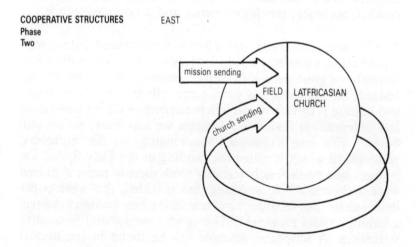

COOPERATIVE STRUCTURES
Phase Two

EAST

mission sending

FIELD

LATFRICASIAN CHURCH

church sending

relationship between Paul, Peter and Apollos in the Corinthian church:

> Now I beseech you, brethren, by the name of our Lord Jesus Christ, that ye all speak the same thing, and that there be no divisions among you; but that ye be perfectly joined together in the same mind and in the same judgment. For it hath been declared unto me of you, my brethren, by them which are of the house of Chloe, that there are contentions among you. Now this I say, that everyone of you saith, I am of Paul; and I of Apollos; and I of Cephas; and I of Christ. Is Christ divided? Was Paul crucified for you? Or were ye baptized in the name of Paul? I thank God that I baptized none of you, but Crispus and Gaius; lest any should say that I had baptized in mine own name. And I baptized also the household or Stephanas; besides, I know not whether I baptized any other. For Christ sent me not to baptize, but to preach the gospel: not with wisdom of words, lest the cross of Christ should be made of none effect. (1 Cor. 1:10-17)
> For while one saith, I am of Paul; and another, I am of Apollos; are ye not carnal? Who then is Paul, and who is Apollos, but ministers of whom ye believed, even as the Lord gave to every man? I have planted, Apollos watered; but God gave the increase. So then neither is he that planteth any thing, neither he that watereth; but God that giveth the increase. Now he that planteth and he that watereth are one: and every man shall receive his own reward according to his own labour. For we are labourers together with God: ye are God's husbandry, ye are God's building. (1 Cor. 3:4-9)
> According to the grace of God which is given unto me, as a wise masterbuilder, I have laid the foundation, and another buildeth thereon. But let every man take heed how he buildeth thereupon. (1 Cor. 3:10)

EPILOGUE

Effective and solidified structure can really accomplish an amazing multiplicity of tasks. No matter how many resources we may have, unless these are exploited and utilized to the fullest extent, they are nothing but weeds on the roadsides or gravel on dry riverbeds.

If the tremendous heavenly resources which so far have been left untouched in the wilderness of the Two Thirds World were to be exploited, only then could East and West be fully and unreservedly united to achieve successfully a great missionary purpose in this generation.

1. One of the basic elements of this united missionary task

5

Packaging or Partnership:
A Model for True Church Growth

SIMON BARRINGTON-WARD

In many parts of the world church, people are moving 'out from under' inherited or imposed institutions to discover new ways of worship and of life together. You find them in informal gatherings, house-meetings and cells—settings somewhat removed from the ordinary activities of the church. They may be in groups like the communal farm I visited in Japan, where rural workers from many countries developed their skills – above all in relationships – as they worked together under Dr Takaki's inspiration. You will find them in renewal meetings: whether among Aboriginal Australian villagers meeting in the open air to sing or pray, in a youth camp in Calcutta, or in an afternoon gathering in a large church in Kigali, Rwanda.

At once you realize that the movements which have stirred and spread the church, exploding and expanding from within, have seldom, if ever, come from the top, or worked their way through the formal structure downwards and outwards. From the beginning they have been spontaneous uprushings of the life of the Spirit, moving at will among particular people in particular places.

STRUCTURE NEEDS COMMUNITY

Recently Ralph Winter, one of the Pasadena 'church growth' school, claimed: 'Every Christian tradition . . . will gradually lose the spiritual vitality with which it may have begun' [1]. He sees that, whereas the Roman Catholic tradition could make up for this becomes one expression and instrument of a missionary spirit which exists in the local churches and in the church universal. The society becomes a kind of sign or sacrament of the church as a whole, just as the society, by the particular commitment and dedication of its members, should point the local church itself to its own essential character as a committed community.

The voluntary society, like the order, becomes the servant of the local church, standing for and embodying the openness of that church to the kingdom. And international fellowships and teams of dedicated people must seek to witness to the true nature both of the gospel and of the church which they go out to bring to life, and, in unevangelized areas, to bring into being. Indeed, for a recent Benedictine study of monastic life, 'the meaning of monasticism is to be sought in the centre rather than on the periphery of the church's life' [4]. The church needs such communities, not to live its life for it, but to show how it should be living that life and to encourage it so to live. Orders, missionary fellowships, or whatever they may be, can foster the renewal of local congregations and encourage cross-cultural mission. They will provide one means among many others. Sometimes, reciprocally, they may themselves receive powerful stimulus and reinvigoration from the local church.

The present evangelistic opportunity, the needs of the surrounding world, the pressure of world-wide poverty and injustice, the universal hunger for direction and meaning, all demand a total transformation of the church. They demand vigorous lay-participation, a new quality of compassion and of evangelisitc witness, a readiness on the part of every one of us to attempt to move across cultural frontiers. All new structures must now be judged, in Ross Kinsler's words, 'by their effectiveness in allowing and enabling people themselves to discover and express their faith' [5].

For such a purpose, special 'ginger' groups are needed as much now as ever they have been: groups which, like the early evangelicals of the eighteenth century, like the Clapham sect, like Charles Simeon's young men, like the Tractarian priests in London's dockland in the late nineteenth century, will discover special bonds and special spiritual resources for special tasks.

Alongside the movement of Partners in Mission and provincial centralization, we need in the church – as in secular organizations – a deliberate 'un-coupling' of the system so that the centre serves

Taiwan, the Philippines, Korea, Indonesia, and twenty more in India – and with larger associations of such missions forming. In Kenya, diocesan missionary associations, admittedly closely tied to the diocesan structure, are supporting missionaries in their own area, while a newly formed overseas 'mission board' (again a model that suggests almost too much central direction) intends to send Kenyan missionaries overseas. Similarly, in West Africa, the Evangelical Missionary Society, the missionary arm of its parent church, has sent 200 missionary couples to the Maguzawa and Fulani people in the north of Nigeria, as well as to Ghana.

In Latin America, Pentecostal and other Protestant groups have sent out missionaries from their own to other areas: notably the Brazilian Baptists and Assemblies of God. Williams points out the advantages enjoyed by missionaries sent out by a relatively poorer church in a 'mission out of poverty', as he calls it, rather than out of affluence. Juan Carlos Ortiz's church sent three missionary couples to another part of Latin America with three months' support and a one-way ticket. They were to support themselves thereafter, until the church that sprang from their labours was able to take them on. It would be easier for such relatively 'powerless' missionaries to identify with the poor and oppressed, like the early Christian missionary movement. How desperately Western missionary agencies need the stimulus, the corrective, and the restoring of their own integrity which a genuinely interdependent partnership with such Third World groups could give them.

Equally, however, Williams points to the problems faced by such enterprises: lacking often not only the organizational resources, the training and the experience of Western agencies, but also the perception of what such missionary enterprise might entail. One Korean missionary, Chun Chae Ok, has written feelingly of the need for more understanding support than she received[7]. Both she and Williams indicate clearly the need for cooperation with the existing Western movement, for a sharing of staff, finance and information, a real partnership in trust.

COMMUNITY NEEDS STRUCTURE

A proper relationship with an existing church is also wise. A community movement that breaks away entirely from the structures becomes a detached organization on its own, and can missionary to go, and the missionary will depend upon 'the power at his disposal' – to quote a significant phrase of his – and it is simplistic to look at mission overseas as a painfully maturing interchange, as I described it, between ourselves and Christian equals. It must be far more than that, since that is not a way of working which could reach the three billion not yet evangelized. But it is the first, the Great Commission, that get the least attention and needs the most. 'What are we doing about it?' he asks.

It is a fair challenge. He suggests that our society's failure to embark on fresh ventures of cross-cultural evangelism arises from post-imperial guilt. Obviously it is right to criticize inertia, but the essential point is this: partnership is not an alternative to obedience to the Great Commission. It is the only way of responding to it. The primary task is a call for the renewal of the whole church and for its return to the gospel. Westerners cannot seek to bypass other churches by setting up new agencies; rather, Westerners must draw other churches into their fellowship, and those other churches must draw Westerners into their own. We must provoke each other by letters like that of Donald McGavran. Human society is no longer set in static cultural blocks. The whole world is circulating and interpenetrating more and more. What is needed is a renewed, revived, international Christian community with a shared sense of urgency and an acknowledgement of gifts to bring and of gifts to receive. Such a movement would be likely to commend itself internationally by this very quality of interdependence.

A seemingly give-away hint in Donald McGavran's letter is a reference to the power at the disposal of missionaries. I want to ask what he really means by that. Is it a power of the Spirit or a power of numbers? An isolated missionary in Khartoum, for example, sees new forms of church and gospel emerging around him; sees a movement that is being led by others; sees initiatives being taken by those to whom he is introducing the gospel; sees leadership spontaneously growing. It is not through an army of evangelists coming from outside and dominating the enterprise. The mystery of inter-dependence and of true sharing may indeed be the heart of the new evangelism that is to emerge in our time. Bodies of evangelists from the West, operating separately from the Third World Church, have come under considerable Third World criticism of late. We can hear a Third World voice if we listen to the letter of an Asian friend, secretary of the Christian Council in his area, commenting on a particular development which involves some Western agencies:

the *status quo*, and no doubt that explains much of what we have failed to do. But I think that at present the call is to discover a relationship in which we can speak to each other truthfully and openly. I know that within the next two or three years the opportunity might come of responding in partnership with the Church of Sierra Leone to the challenge which Donald McGavran has put to us – but perhaps we should rather have put it to them. If Donald McGavran had not written in this strain, it could have been that the opportunity would not have been presented so vividly and clearly. We must be immensely grateful to him for this, as for much else. But our response must be a shared response. It must be a response which draws in Christians in Sierra Leone and revives, renews and opens up both us and them. It must be a venture within which those in Sierra Leone and those in CMS discover each other afresh.

In justification of much that he says, Donald McGavran points to St Paul's missionary strategy and activity, seeming to see St Paul as the individual entrepreneur (his word) in mission. Perhaps the very entrepreneurial metaphor is in itself significant, with its overtone of western capitalist individualism. In his fascinating commentary on Romans, F.J. Leenhardt[12] showed Paul not as an isolated individual acting on his own authority (although he certainly had a deep sense of his own calling which he received from no man), but as an apostle working at his finished work within the Jerusalem area, taking the opinion, the blessing and the backing of the Jerusalem church with profound seriousness, and, when later he was about to take to Jerusalem the fruit of the generosity of the Christian communities founded among the Gentiles, being conscious that he had fulfilled a task upon which he could now report back in Jerusalem. The original leaping-off point of St Paul's work, the church in Antioch, was itself a marvellous mix, a fellowship of the unlike. It was only with the blessing of that community, in obedience to the Holy Spirit, that Paul and Barnabas originally set off together. Although they had considerable independence – the independence of a missionary society, or perhaps today the freedom of a certain kind of missionary 'sodality' – yet they always acted in the closest unity and interdependence with the church in Antioch and reported back to that church in due course. There was, I believe, something of the interdependent character that the Church Missionary Society now has in its relation to the Partnership for World Mission[13] in he describes as the second stage: 'interchurch partnership in mission'. Now this seems to be putting the whole process precisely the wrong way round. The first stage is manifestly where we are beginning to be now: that in which the Western church seeks sensitively and penitently a new self-critical relationship of genuine partnership and trust with its Third World counterparts. This interchurch relationship is primary, and in a way with which Pasadena, it sometime seems, has not yet wholly come to terms. Indeed, all Western churches, societies, orders, movements, still have some way to go in working this through.

The second stage, about to begin, will surely see a new type of international frontier mission emerging, in which the Western societies and churches, no longer dormant, still provide something of the finance, the infra-structure, the organization, and some of the participants. The Third World churches will provide much of the leadership. Teams, part international, part local, shared initiatives, joint training and evaluation, will be launched from bases not necessarily in the West. The participants will be ready, above all, at whatever cost, to incarnate the gospel they seek to convey – a gospel which necessarily carries with it profound social and political implications.

Here is no divide between institutional church and voluntary community. The instrument may well be a new international partnership of voluntary groupings sprouting from within many varied churches. The institutional churches from which such groups arise, and in the areas to which they go, will be ready to authenticate and to 'earth' them by their encouragement and support. Similarly, the churches which such groups help to bring into being will in turn free their own members from such special communities. Between orders or societies and churches there can be internationally a reciprocal sense of responsibility and of mutual communication. The communities stimulate and inspire the structures. In Christ they both need and serve each other.

NOTES

(1) Ralph D. Winter, 'Protestant Mission Societies: the American Experience', *Missiology* 7, 1979, p.140
(2) Lesslie Newbigin, *Context and Conversion* (London: CMS, 1978), pp.12-13.
(3) *Ibid.*, p.11
(4) David Rees *et al.*, *Consider Your Call: A Theology of Monastic Life Today* (London: SPCK, 1978), p.6
(5) Quoted from an unpublished paper

6

Agenda for Missions in the Eighties and Nineties: A Discussion Starter

VINAY SAMUEL AND CHRIS SUGDEN

THE NATIONAL CHURCH BY-PASS

Many of the developments in mission since 1945, and some of the strategies mapped out for the future, by-pass the national church.

By 'national church' we refer to visible expressions of the body of Christ who are independent in finance and policy within the context of their national setting. These expressions are fellowships of groups who nurture one another in the faith through worship and service together. They can be geographically local expressions, or non-residential groups of common interests rooted in one national area.

We draw a distinction between these national expressions which are independent financially and in policy matters, and those which are subsidiaries of multi-national mission boards. Those in the second group have national leaders but their existence in a country is dependent on outside leaders and fund raising. Since 1945 there has been a proliferation of such Christian institutions. In earlier years they had complete missionary leadership and home boards controlled matter of finance and policy. Leadership in the 'host' country may now be in national hands but the effective power in decision-making lies with organizations outside the country.

Our thesis is that in many areas these multi-national mission agencies are actually preventing the effective mission of the Gospel in the contexts where they operate.

THE INAUTHENTIC GOSPEL

Unfortunately it is possible to identify a reduced, inauthentic Gospel in the proclamation of many mission agencies and organizations. The Gospel is reduced to a message to believe, a slogan to proclaim. Such a Gospel is inauthentic because it is not *incarnate*, or contextually clothed. It therefore does not have the power of God to transform human life.

Such a Gospel reflects the spirit of the consumer society. The goal is to make the Gospel as easily and as widely available as possible. It is essentially for individuals, and therefore studies are made of individual psychological needs. The Gospel message is presented to meet those needs; it does not address the wider social context in which the individuals live. The goal and method is strikingly similar to the marketing of Coca Cola. Such a goal and method, unrelated to the incarnate Gospel, cheapens the message and dehumanizes its hearers and promoters. The hearers of the Gospel are not treated as individuals in their context, but only as impersonal universal man: Coca Cola is not interested in your cultural make-up, only in the fact that you get thirsty. The bearers of the Gospel are treated only in terms of their psychological needs of guilt, fear, anxiety, loneliness; their social existence in their society (whether they are employed or not, receive just treatment or not, have liberty or not) is ignored; Coca Cola is not interested whether you are an oppressor or one of the oppressed, as long as you can afford to pay for the drink. Neither is Coca Cola interested in the social conditions of the country. In India, thousands of villages have Coca Cola available, but not drinking water.

INCARNATION IN THE BODY OF CHRIST

Where does the incarnation of the Gospel of the incarnation take place? It cannot take place in one international model which is valid for all cultures. That would ignore the model of Jesus who was incarnate in one culture, and the distinctives of each culture. There must be contextual models in each culture of what the incarnate Gospel is for that situation. Such modelling can be done only by the Body of Christ in that specific context.

The Body of Christ in each of its national expressions is to incarnate the Gospel in that context. The Church should model

MISSION AS STRUGGLE

The mission of the Church is to be set in the midst of the context of the world and the particular context in which the church is set. If we consider the work of God only in that context and our criterion is growth, then we will define mission in terms of fruitfulness, as the growing and expanding fruit of the Gospel. However, evil is also at work in the world. The focus of God's activity is to present every man complete in the image of Christ, and the focus of evil's activity is to destroy that image in every man and deform every man into the image of the evil one. God's work is humanization in Christ, and the work of the evil one is dehumanization. Evil is not only at work in cults and witchcraft, but also in the sweatshops of Hong Kong and the paddy fields of Andhra Pradesh, as men are forced to work like animals on insufficient wages. In a world where both God and evil are at work, mission is a struggle to establish and extend God's Kingdom, to present man complete in the image of Christ, in conflict with the activities of the evil one. It is struggle not in the sense that we struggle in our own unaided efforts; it is struggle in the sense that Jesus and Paul describe Christian ministry and mission, as following the pattern of death and resurrection, redemptive suffering and the ministry of suffering servanthood. The effectiveness of Christian mission cannot be measured in terms of numerical growth or improved financial statistics. Effective Christian mission includes losing oneself, suffering, failure, trouble, doubt, enemies, hurt, persecution and death. The resurrection tells us that these are God's channels of life.

In practical terms such struggle against evil may involve the church in a national context in encouraging and joining groups which seek to make oppressed people aware of their rights, and non-violently acting with them in the strength of a united stand against those who would exploit them. This process is technically known as the process of struggle for justice, and the Church in its mission of struggle may well have to take part in such struggles for justice as it incarnates the Gospel.

Christian learning must take place in the setting of mission as struggle. This must be education not of an elite but of the whole people of God. The biblical theme 'every member ministry' demands that Christian education be available to every member. This goal in Christian education will devolve power to the people.

N.F.M.—E

products as widely as possible. They direct their energy and efforts to efficient packaging and distribution in order to promote cheap availability of their product. However the Third World is littered with examples of the devastation caused by inappropriate products expertly marketed by multi-nationals. Nestlé skilfully marketed ready-mix baby milk to illiterate mothers in Africa; the mothers replaced nature's purest food supply with baby-mix made with the local polluted water, causing disease and death. The multinationals wanted to market their product at all costs, and created an artificial sense of need in the consumer unrelated to any real needs.

Some strategies for Christian mission are based on a global organization promoting a clearly articulated verbal message. The goal is to make this message as widely available as possible, preferably to people who have no relationship with national Christian groups (E3 evangelism). If the Gospel message is reduced to individual salvation as a cure for loneliness, it will not meet India's needs. For in India's strong family society, the loneliness that characterizes (and is a product of?) Western industrialized society is not such a pronounced problem as in the West. A non-incarnate verbal universal message by-passes incarnation in a context, by-passes the needs of the whole context, creates its own needs and subverts the mission of the Gospel.

CHURCHES AS DISTRIBUTION CENTRES

In the multi-national strategy, local centres are bases for distribution. Even if they are production centres, they manufacture a product identical to the master copy and distribute it locally. The criterion of their performance is whether they distribute the product effectively. If they do not, then the franchise is moved to a new company.

We discern this same spirit in the ecclesiology (or lack of it) in current mission strategies. The church is defined as a distribution centre. If the national church is not an effective distribution centre for the product of the mission agency, then it is by-passed, and the agency creates its own church, its own distribution system.

global scale. We find airlines in the hotel and car rental business; we find Mitsubishi and Philips dividing the electronics business between them. We discern similar trends in the Christian world. Relief and development agencies move into evangelism and church planting, theological education and leadership training, mission research and literature publication. We find agencies dividing up the market between them and regarding particular territories as their own sphere of influence. The recent indignation of one Western agency that another agency had moved in to set up an headquarters in its 'patch' can be matched only by the unexpressed indignation of 'recipient' countries that the original agency presumes to tell them what they can and cannot do in their own country. We find dubious policies being allowed in order to keep ahead of other competitors in the market. We know that one aid agency is now a channel for government funds, in a bid to ensure stability for massively increased budgets.

EVALUATION

In the business world there is one law. Profits. Profit is the only criterion which shareholders are interested in; and they alone are in a position to hold multi-nationals to account. What a multi-national does to the structures of justice and humanity in a country is not its concern. No controls have yet been worked out for multi-nationals, and their own vested interests and declared goals make them quite impervious, if not hostile, to criticism.

We find that multi-national mission agencies find it very hard to listen to critical questions raised from Scripture about their activities. They have their own limited agenda and pleased that they must fulfil their supporters' expectations. When it was suggested at a recent international conference that relief and development agencies try to educate First World supporters about the real situation in the Third World, it was seriously suggested that 90% of the income of the agency would disappear if this happened.

There are vested interests in theological positions. Through reading *Kids and the Kingdom*[1], by John Inchley, a Scripture Union children's worker of vast experience, we are coming to realise that it may be more scriptural to regard children as belonging

7

Church and Mission in the Age of Multi-National Corporations: Some Reflections

THEODORE WETTACH

PRELIMINARY REMARKS

Our age is marked by two contradictory tendencies. On the one hand it can be observed that more and more people – mainly of the younger generation – are against all institutions and try to live as Christians in fellowship with Jesus without any institutions. In this way they develop thoroughly new, spontaneous ways of fellowship which do, however, show some patterns. It can be observed that they are then looking for fellowship and safety in small groups.

In contrast to this is the emergence, especially in the Western world, of an undetermined number of trans-national and multinational ecclesiastical and missionary organizations. The first 'generation' of federations consisted of Christians who remained or wanted to remain members of their parishes but united for particular tasks like prayer and evangelism. Among these I would number the Evangelical Alliances, the YMCA and Christian Students Movement. The World Council of Churches originally was a loose alliance of Christian churches but it soon developed its own dynamics and extended its central office more and more.

Then there are also the denominational world alliances: the Lutheran World Federation, World Alliance of Reformed Churches and so on; and in our own time we observe the increasing esteem of the denominational heritages.

In response to the theological tendencies of the ecumenical

churches increased and grew up – after some teething troubles and puberty symptoms – and developed an independence which sometimes came too fast in the eyes of the European and American mother churches.

The State Church structures in most of the European churches did not allow direct missionary work in other countries. Therefore missionary societies were necessary in order to realize the world missionary task of the churches. Added to this is the fact that among the national churches themselves, the church has not only to be reformed but also to be evangelized, so that the church in its entirety can never be a missionary church. But even the Free and Confessing churches participate in the servant-shape of the church of Jesus Christ in the world. Despite their short-comings, all churches and Christian communities are living. Our Lord wants to use weak people in order to prepare the coming of his Kingdom. All churches announce that Christ forgives sins and makes a new start possible. The variety of the church's ways of service, together with the inevitable impact upon it of events of world history, obliged it to find again and again new forms and structures for mission work. These forms were legitimate as long as they were serving the church and aimed at the church. Mission organizations are therefore part of the church only as far as they take part in the life of that church and as far as they see themselves as a task of the church, integrating and submitting themselves to the church.

Only in so far as the mission understands itself as a task given to a church, does it remain faithful towards the missionary command given by Christ to his church. But it must also be said that missionary work can meet this command only in so far as it has got the freedom, the mobility and the potential to cross frontiers.

A spirit of true integration with the churches, and freedom of obedience to the Lord of the mission, are, to say the least, en-dangered within the new multinational mission corporations. I can hardly detect a church character among many of these worldwide organizations which devote themselves to such things as trans-denominational evangelism, refugee relief work, and the illegal passing on of Christian literature within the Communist world, and which are not a legitimate part of the church in a certain place or country.

THE MISSION OF THE EVANGELICAL MOVEMENT TODAY

The evangelical movement was and is a renewal and evangelism movement within the existing churches. It prevented the churches from becoming immovable and they found new life through the strength of God's Spirit and through the power of God's Word. I am convinced that this service of the German Pietistic movement was necessary for missionary work of the church. It is a service which can no longer be rendered if the strength of the evangelical movement goes into trans-national organizations and therefore cannot be used any longer for building up the church of Jesus Christ. I am also convinced that the evangelical movement urgently needs this frame. The international organizations run the risk of becoming church-like institutions without being either churches, or even part of the church of Jesus Christ in the whole world. Without the evangelical movement the existing churches, the old churches of the Reformation as well as the Free churches, run the risk of becoming inflexible and forgetting the missionary command.

intimate fellowship with God. And a new movement is knocking at the doors of evangelical consciousness; borrowing the title of Christopher Sugden's book, we may call it *radical discipleship*. This describes the growing awareness that Christ means us to take the social, economic and political implications of the Gospel no less seriously than we take the 'spiritual' implications. In theory, there is the closest connection between these three movements. *Revival* and *radical discipleship* are concerned with what God is doing in the world (he is saving it, and in Christ remaking it); *renewal* is concerned with how he is doing it (through the Holy Spirit and in the Church). But the sad truth is that for many Christians these complementary descriptions of God's work appear to be competitive with one another, or may take place without each other.

2. THE CHURCH, THE NEW COMMUNITY

We have seen that both witness and service are essential ingredients of the Christian mission; and God has committed mission primarily to the whole Body of the Church, and only secondarily to individuals whom he may call and equip for any particular work. In this and the following sections, we atttempt to draw out some of the consequences of this view, and to see how renewed Christianity should set about its God-given tasks.

a. The Communitarian Understanding of the Church

Although God has used renewal to emphasize the importance of the community, individualism remains the predominant thought-world to which Westerners easily revert. This is the reason why many Western evangelicals feel uneasy when they hear tales of 'people movements' and group conversions in other cultural settings: they surmise that faith which originates in such a fashion is not 'personal'; it is a mere going along with the crowd.

Personal contact with the Kikuyu tribe in Kenya has shown me that they do not regard the individual as the human 'unit of account'. The individual is perceived as a member of his extended family, clan and tribe. The continuity of the social unit extends through successive generations, including both deceased ancestors and unborn children. The links between generations are secured by a

In seeking God's guidance in the exercise of the Church's power in the economic, political and social spheres, we quickly exhaust the New Testament's direct teaching (e.g. the apostolic community in Jerusalem; the instruction to regard the state's authority as God-given; and conjectures about what Paul might have said to Philemon had he been discussing the institution of slavery). The New Testament Church was virtually powerless to affect, save by its prayers, the large matters of economics and politics which today fall within the scope of the Church's power, and therefore our responsibility.

In the Old Testament, however, we do see the people of God exercising political power; consequently those with a strong interest in 'orthopraxis' have turned increasingly to the Old Testament for guidance.

However, we need to exercise hermeneutical restraint if we are to recognise the true usefulness of the Old Testament's witness. The Old Testament describes the social conditions within the people of God and not the relationship between the covenant people and the outside world.

Although God's purpose of blessing the whole of mankind through Israel was apparent from the moment that he first spoke to Abram (Gen. 12:3), nevertheless in the Old Testament the mission was fulfilled simply by Israel's being an example to the nations, showing forth the glory of God (Ezek. 36:23).

In the New Testament, however, the nature of mission has changed. The frontier of Israel has been thrown down and the grace of God goes out to seek and save men where they are.

This alteration has a double effect on Christian social responsibility. On the one hand, it calls us to apply God's standards and to make his appeal outside the boundaries of the Church. Although God's standards have always been binding on men (cf. Rom. 1:18ff, Am. 2:1), the whole work of God has now flooded the world. But on the other hand, it requires us to impose God's standards in a new context – among the very people whom we are trying to call into the circle of the grace which has come to us.

These two factors – the primary interest of the Old Testament in relations within the people of God, and the altered nature of mission – will affect the way we apply the Old Testament to current issues in service. The universal scope of New Testament mission implies that the Old Testament social message also has universal relevance. Radical discipleship has, however, not yet development workers. Such workers are chosen by their parishes and are given two months' residential training. They form a vital link between government services (which often seem somewhat remote from village life) and the ordinary farmer or housewife, especially in disseminating information. The crucial point is this. The work is being carried out *in partnership with*, not independently from, the 'spiritual' work of the diocese. CCS staff, many of who are experts in their field on secondment from government services, are (as far as possible) genuinely committed Christians. The most visible link between the 'service' and 'witness' aspects of the Diocese's mission is the Diocesan training centre, St Andrew's Institute for Mission and Evangelism.

St Andrew's is a theological and development resource centre. Training courses are held simultaneously for health and agriculture workers, and for thirty or more students, training for the ordained ministry. The resulting cross-fertilization leads to clergy who take a positive interest in development, and also to health and agriculture workers being converted or deepened in their spiritual life.

CCS is not set up as a bait to draw the unwary to the Gospel. It has its own goals, determined by a Christian view of a desirable development which includes involving local people in decision-making about the patterns of development in their area. If not a single person was converted through CCS activities, it would not be a 'wasted effort', any more than Jesus' work in healing disease was rendered useless when those whom he healed proved thankless or disobedient (Lk. 17:17; Mk. 1:45). To obey God in this service is already glorifying to him.

But in fact, CCS does have an impact on both evangelism and growth in Christian maturity. Today, most churches in the fertile parts of the Diocese are partnered with congregations in the arid areas, arranging exchange visits of evangelistic teams, and supplying food aid at times of shortage. The Bishop was recently greeted rather emotionally by members of a local health committee with: 'If it were not for your work some of us would not be alive today!' Perhaps the most convincing sign that service has not cut the nerve of witness is provided by statistics: between 1975 and 1981, over 70 new congregations were established; and in the period between 1979 and 1980 alone, in areas of the Diocese with a total population of 700,000, at least 12,700 people are known to have been baptized.

N.F.M.—F

in fact meet with considerable success. Unfortunately, the New Testament never goes into detail on how any case like this was handled in apostolic times.

The best solution lies in the structures of the local church. Any suggestion of separation in the church, especially in contexts which include the racial, touches a raw nerve in many Christian communities. For this reason we must insist that the initiative for establishing such a separate group within the church must always belong to the members of those groups. The reason for permitting such separation is always to allow the potentially 'oppressed' people group to safeguard its identity against the potential 'oppressor's' cultural imperialism. They have chosen the separation, not had it thrust upon them. In the case of a church which has a large membership from one group and a small membership from a second group, the onus lies on the larger group to become sensitive to the needs of the smaller, to modify its own conduct and outlook, and constantly to seek ways of joining in closer fellowship.

The renewal movement has enormous contributions to make to the successful establishment of churches which embrace cultural or linguistic diversity in this fashion. The recognition (which renewal has brought) that 'new wine needs new wineskins' has eatablished a generation of Christians resolved to sit loose to particular culturally-determined expressions of worship, so that the Holy Spirit may suggest new vehicles for devotion to God. They also recognize that he may say the same things and meet with the same response under the cultural forms of another people group.

In this way the ground is prepared for deep mutual acceptance and trust between Christians from different groups, such that none feels threatened by the foreignness of the other.

So far we have considered 'people groups' which are defined by criteria which are unchanging or subject only to slow change – criteria such as race, language, social class, culture. However, in Western societies there is a proliferation of what *almost* amount to 'people groups', defined by shared interests – or other factors which are ephemeral, or which do not automatically affect all members of a family. There are undoubtedly people whose major interest in life is related to organizations such as Gingerbread (for single parents) or the Campaign for Nuclear Disarmament. The increasing importance of single-issue politics will make such groups even more numerous and significant.

This fact creates an opportunity for mission which the Church in Kenya – not surprisingly, for it contains an implied condemnation of the manner in which Kenyan Christians are discharging their mission. It becomes all the more galling when these maverick evangelists come from countries with notably lower conversion rates and church attendance figures than Kenya! Within Kenya demarcation disputes have arisen in recent years as the old missionary 'comity' arrangements have begun to break down. As Christians migrate around the country, their denominations tend to follow them. Occasionally this extension of existing churches across old frontiers has met with hostility and resentment.

We need a criterion to distinguish between responding to a God-given call and usurping a work which rightfully belongs to someone else.

In the New Testament, the pattern of the discharge of the Church's mission was almost as complex as it is today. Those who in Antioch preached the Gospel to the Greek also (Acts 11:20) did not wait for anyone to authorize their action. Philip (Acts 8:26) undertook an important piece of evangelistic work at the prompting of an angel – possibly to the surprise of the other apostles, since he abandoned a promising mission in Samaria in order to do so. On the other hand, Saul and Barnabas were set apart for their work through the agency of the Church at Antioch (Acts 13:2).

In the course of Paul's ministry, he met and occasionally clashed with other Christian missionaries and leaders. However, he never complained simply because they had trespassed on his territory. Paul saw his own responsibility as being to cover the ground rapidly with an evangelistic sweep, planting churches as fast as possible (2 Cor. 10:16, Rom. 15:20). He recognised and happily accepted that others, with complementary responsibility, would work alongside him or after him (1 Cor. 3:10).

On two occasions we see Paul moving to someone else's territory: when writing Romans, and when visiting Jerusalem (Acts 21). Concerning Romans, the apparently diffident tone of 1:8-15 (and to a lesser extent of 15:14-33) has been variously explained; but it is at least consistent with the interpretation that Paul feels himself to be writing to a church for which others bear the primary responsibility. In Acts 21, there is of course no contradiction between the elders' request (v.23f) and Paul's theology. However, it is of interest that they joined their request with a reference to the letter of the Jerusalem council (Acts 15:23-29, 21:25). A comparison of Paul's letter (e.g. Rom. 14:14, 2 Cor. 8:4) and the extension of the 'Good Samaritan' principle: that the person who comes upon a case of need has the primary duty of meeting that need, whether or not he considers himself to be a specialist or ideally equipped for the task. When an agency is already at work meeting a particular need, then unless it chooses to ask another group to take over its responsiblities, it should be regarded as having the first claim. Offers of help should be channelled through it.

This principle holds good even when the agency nominally engaged in the work appears to be neglecting its duties. The Lord himself is both gentle and patient with his incompetent servants (Is. 40:11, 42:3); he does not measure their potential effectiveness by their human resources (Dt. 7:7, Zech. 4:6); and he is more ready to strengthen than to bypass an agency which is proving weak (Heb. 12:12-13, Rev. 3:2). We are too quick to assume that the Lord has carried out his ultimate threat of 'removing the lampstand' of a spiritually shaky church. In the present generation there is still a risk that the Spirit's gifts of leadership and evangelism given in newly autonomous Third World churches may be compromised by interference from Western mission agencies. In the next generation it may well be the rapidly growing churches in Africa, Asia and Latin America who despise the ineffectuality of the Western Churches and march in uninvited to do what the West is so plainly incapable of doing for itself.

Perhaps in a few cases the existing church in a certain place is so lackadaisical, corrupt, or prejudiced that it ignores a crying need on its own doorstep, and faithfulness to the Gospel positively demands outside intervention. But such cases may be rarer than we think. Our perceptions of acute need may sometimes be based more on Western culture than on the Gospel. A little restraint may become the source of blessing.

Our Lord Jesus Christ prayed that the disciples 'may be one, as we are' (John 17:11). He did not pray merely that the twelve disciples might be one but also that *those who believe in him as a result of their ministry* might also be one. The basis of this unity is the unity which already exists between the Father and Son, expressed in John 17:20-21.

> I do not pray for these only, but also for those who believe in me through their word, that they may be one; even as Thou, O Father, art in me, and I in Thee, that they may also be in us, so that the world may believe that Thou hast sent me.

Jesus in this prayer asks that the oneness of all believers should resemble that oneness which exists between the Father and the Son. Jesus takes the unity of the persons of the Trinity to be the model and the foundation of the unity of believers. Though the unity of believers can never be *identical* with the unity of the persons of the Trinity, nevertheless, the believers can take the oneness of the Father and the Son as a pattern of their expected unity. The purpose of such unity among believers is that 'the world may believe that Thou hast sent me'. The main purpose of Church unity is to demonstrate to the world that Jesus Christ is indeed the Son of God.

A faithful exegesis of this passage does not support the idea that ecumenical organizational oneness is a cardinal virtue which supersedes all other virtues. The unity of which this text speaks is essentially personal and spiritual, in accordance with the supreme analogy of the union of the Father and the Son.

b) Exhortation to maintain the unity of the Spirit in the bond of peace

> I, therefore, a prisoner of the Lord, beg you to lead a life worthy of the calling to which you have been called, with all lowliness and meekness, with patience, forbearing one another in love, eager to maintain the unity of the Spirit in the bond of peace. There is one body and one Spirit, just as you were called to one hope, that belongs to your call, one Lord, one faith, one baptism, one God and Father of us all, who is above all and through all and in all. (Eph. 4:1-6.)

This is the most important Pauline passage on the unity and diversity of the Church.

In Romans 12:4-5, St Paul uses the same analogy: 'For as in one body we have many members, and all the members do not have the same function, so we, though many, are one body in Christ, and individually members one of another.' In expounding this passage, C. K. Barrett sees the setting of the argument of one body in Christ as being not so much sacramental as eschatological. 'It was the body of Christ which died in the messianic affliction and rose to life in the age to come; those who are to share in this process must enter into and become part of the body of Christ.'[(2)].

Presumably we become part of the body of Christ by baptism (Rom. 6:3-11, Gal. 3:27), and in the eucharistic meal we participate in the body of Christ. 'The bread which we break, is it not a participation in the body of Christ? Because there is one bread, we who are many are one body, for we all partake of the one bread.' (1 Cor. 10:16b-17). These considerations make the importance of unity quite clear, as well as the dreadful consequences of the lack of it. Alan Richardson says emphatically that 'there can be no Christians who are not members of the one body of Christ and therefore of one another, so that to be out of communion with other Christians is to be out of communion with Christ'.[(3)]

d) One Flock, One Shepherd

> And I have other sheep, that are not of this flock; I must bring them also and they will heed my voice. So there shall be one flock, one shepherd. (John 10:16).

The Old Testament frequently uses the metaphor of Israel as the flock of which Yahweh is the shepherd and ruler. Our Lord thought of his own mission as that of a shepherd sent to gather the Israel of God. The above passage stresses the unity of the Church in God in its missionary activity. The mission of the Church to the Gentiles is an activity of Christ himself who wants to find other sheep which at the present time are not in the fold of his flock. When he brings them, they become part of the one flock belonging to the one shepherd. Consequently, the flock of Christ will no longer be confined to believers from among the Jews.

e) Summary – the unity of the Church

In this section we have attempted to expound the key biblical passages on the unity of the Church. It has clearly been emphasized varieties of service, but the same Lord; and there are varieties of workings but it is the same God who inspires them all in everyone. (1 Cor. 12:4-6.)

Christians differ from each other not only in their natural make-up but also in the spiritual gifts distributed to each. Paul goes out of his way to remind Christians that the gifts of the Holy Spirit are meant for the building of the body of Christ and should not be used for bringing divisions in the Church. Indeed, in chapter 13, he teaches that *Love* is much more important as a spiritual grace, and any spiritual gift exercised without love is of no benefit.

The variety of the gifts of the Holy Spirit should therefore be used for the building of the body of Christ. It is a great pity that in recent years the gifts of the Holy Spirit have been used more to divide the Church in certain quarters than to build the body of Christ. In exercising the spiritual gifts God has given to the members of the Church, we should promote unity in the bond of peace.

b) **Diversity of theologies**

The fact that the Church is one does not mean that there should be no *plurality of opinion* and theological understanding. The early Christians were not necessarily of one mind in all theological issues; yet Christians clung tenaciously to the conviction that there is one Lord, one faith, one baptism, one God who is Father of all (Eph. 4:5-6). They gathered regularly for the Lord's Supper, supported the weak, and gave hospitality to freelance evangelists and other Christians who came their way.

It is possible that the first Hellenic Christians, such as Stephen and Philip, took a theological view of the Jewish Law which differed considerably from that of the Jewish apostles. Stephen was accused of 'speaking words against this holy place' in order to 'change the customs which Moses delivered to us' (Acts 6:13-14).

> The early Church in fact knew different 'theologies' but the factions did not for that accuse each other of heresy. It was not just orthopraxis (agreement in matters of practical Christian conduct) which held the community together; but Christians looked more closely at orthodoxy (right belief), only when dangerous false teaching – coupled with false unchristian behaviour – threatened the community's stablility.[6]

The pioneer missionaries from Europe and North America tended, by and large, to impose a structure of ministries upon the new Christian communities in the missionary areas. Some of the structures imposed, whether Episcopalian, Presbyterian, Pentecostal or Congregational, may not have necessarily fitted the concept of government and leadership of the community. As Gustav Aulen says, 'The principle is always that the organization must be of such a character that under various conditions it serves in the best possible manner as an instrument of the gospel for the establishment of the fellowship.'[8]

d) **Diversity in worship**

There is nothing which can restrict the work of the Holy Spirit more than imposing a uniform style of worship which gives no room for individual believers or the local congregation to experiment in new patterns of worship or liturgy as the Spirit may lead them.

The Anglican Church in Africa inherited the Prayer Book written in AD 1662 in English language which was translated literally into local African languages. The Prayer Book has important principles of worship, but leaves no room for including African expressions and useful traditional elements in worship. Attempts are now being made to use those important principles of worship as a basis of having the Prayer Book enriched with elements of African traditions and culture. As John Mbiti says:

> Romanism, Canterburyism and Athenism in Africa are on temporary visas. Christianity is on a permanent term as a 'Mwananchi' [the Swahili term for 'citizen'] in Africa, and it must be enriched from within and not from outside. For too long we have sung borrowed hymns from Europe and America. Now we are beginning to realise that these important hymns have nearly become theologically all extinct. The more we continue to sing them, the nearer we draw to extinguishing the freshness of the Christian faith in Africa. We must allow our rich heritage to make a contribution to Christianity . . . We can add nothing to the gospel, for this is an eternal gift of God; but Christianity is always a beggar seeking for food and drink, cover and shelter from the cultures and times it encounters in its never-ending journey and wanderings.[9]

e) **Conclusion**

The unity of the Christian Church does not therefore mean

and yet there are about twelve different denominations working in this area. The report of a recent survey of unreached peoples of Kenya strongly recommends cooperation of Christian churches in an effort to reach the Digo.

There needs to be dialogue between Christian workers for mutual encouragement, increased understanding of how to reach the Digo, and opportunity to pool resources so as to increase effectiveness. The Digo will not be won to Christ by an isolated effort.[12]

(ii) *Disunity hinders spiritual renewal.* In certain Christian circles it is firmly assumed that nothing good can come from Rome, and so everything connected with Rome is suspect. When the Holy Spirit starts to renew the Roman Church, we would therefore not bother to find out what is happening in that Church.

It would be a very sad thing if evangelicals were to remain stubbornly inflexible at a time when the Catholic Church was constantly summoning its members to seek repentance, reconciliation and intensified dialogue with other Churches.[13]

(iii) *Disunity hinders and destroys fellowship.*

Behold, how good and pleasant it is when brothers dwell in unity. (Psalm 133:1.)

In any given locality, whatever their denominations and backgrounds, Christians ought to live together in unity. For that is not only good, but also pleasant. God's people are *blessed* when they dwell together in unity. But when there are divisions within the church, our fellowship, prayer, evangelism and encouragement are destroyed.

Each little group could benefit immeasurably from the others; yet still the separation persists. No wonder God is hesitant about blessing their individual efforts. No wonder the impact on the rest of the town is negligible.

What about those missionaries from some churches of recent history who missed the scramble for Africa last century, and now come to Kenya heavily loaded by electronic equipment, to impress natives in darkest Africa and win them not to Christ but to their electronically sophisticated fellowship? The natives they try to reach are already baptized and belong to a local Church, Now they are recognition.

Secondly we need to repent of the wrong attitudes we have harboured against other Christians, our lack of love and our failure to listen to one another.

Thirdly we need to establish united prayer meetings and fellowship within the same locality. We also need to work together for spiritual renewal, which brings fresh love for Jesus; which leads to fresh love for one another.

Fourthly we need to work together in community projects such as evangelistic campaigns, social and political action, development programmes, and so on.

We must also seek to recognise and accept Church membership and ministries. The chief criteria for acceptance of one another as brethren in Christ are personal allegiance to Jesus Christ as Lord and Saviour, and the outward seal of baptism. Even where we may have some doubts about a person's faithfulness to the Lord Jesus, we should be willing to let the 'wheat' and 'tares' grow together until the harvest. We should also recognise the God-given ministries that exist in various strands of the Christian Church. 'If the first apostles had the generosity and wisdom to accept Paul's mission to the Gentiles on the grounds that God was manifestly with him, who are we to reject the ministries of others who are not of our communion?'[14]

Finally the unity of the Church must be based on a faithful proclamation of the gospel of Jesus Christ and the administration of the sacraments as commanded by our Lord. The doctrinal basis for unity must be the unchangeable gospel of Jesus Christ as given in the Scriptures. 'Every denomination and tradition must bend to this God-given revelation. Every viewpoint and structure must bow to the word of God and to the Lordship of Christ. The right interpretation of Scripture calls for much prayer and study, with humble acnowledgement that no one person or denomination has a monopoly of the whole truth of God.'[15] We should be united on the basic truths of the *kerygma*, we should have liberty in questionable points, and, in everything, we should have love.

NOTES

(1)   J.R.W. Stott, *God's New Society, the Message of Ephesians* (Leicester: IVP, 1979), pp. 150-151

(2)   C.K. Barrett, *The Epistles: 1 Corinthians and Romans* (London, 1962)

10

The Church and its Mission and Ministry

W. HAROLD FULLER

1. INTRODUCTION

What should be the *priority* of the Church? What could we term that church's *mission*? What is its *ministry*? Why make any distinction between the mission and ministry of the Church? And what do we mean by the Church anyway?

II. THE CHURCH

A. The Nature of the Church

Using the original Greek word commonly translated as 'church' – *ekklesia* or its equivalent, 'congregation' – can help overcome confusion over the nature of the Church. Therefore in this paper I shall use it directly without translating it or even using italics from this point on.

Ekklesia is neither a building nor an organization. It is a 'calling out' of redeemed people. They constitute a community because they have been born of the Spirit of God. They have been redeemed by the Sovereign King. They are 'the community of the redeemed'.

In the sense that a member of the human race comes into existence by being conceived and born, so a person becomes a member of the ekklesia by being born again. He may be with only a few other believers in a village, but he is a member of the 'congregation' of Christ, worldwide. His membership is automatic when he experiences the new birth.

The ekklesia today is still being 'called out' within a lost world, and therefore continues to bear the responsibility of being 'called unto' the mission of reconciling that lost world to God in Christ Jesus (2 Cor. 5:20). We might assume that no one would contest this, but unfortunately there are other basic misconceptions.

C. The Motivation of the Church

It is the Bible which tells us about man's spiritual condition. Therefore those who do not accept the Bible as the inerrant Word of God resort to human philosophy to define sin, man's spiritual state and his destiny. It is not easy for an unregenerate person (one who has not experienced the new birth) to accept the lost condition of himself and his fellow-beings. He can try to rationalize with one of the following arguments:

1. Man has no immortal soul. Death ends all.
2. Man is not eternally lost. He may be reborn for another chance to earn salvation (reincarnation) or he may be able to change his eternal destiny after death (purgatory), or eventually his soul may be annihilated.
3. Christ's sacrifice automatically redeems all humanity: there is no need for personal regeneration. It is a good thing for us to inform mankind of this, but it is not a necessity.
4. All religions lead to heaven. There is no need to preach the Christian gospel; in fact, to do so is a form of arrogance.
5. Man is not "lost" at all; he is only oppressed by fellow-men. Salvation therefore consists of freeing him from oppression and injustice.[4]

Those who argue along these lines, in order to escape the awesome truth that man without Christ is eternally lost, are unable to comprehend the true redemptive purpose of the ekklesia. They do not know anything of Paul's motivation to fulfil that purpose, that mission:

1. The hopeless condition of man (Rom. 3:9-18)
2. The uniqueness of the Gospel (1 Tim. 2:4-6)
3. The urgency of the task (2 Cor. 5:11)
4. The necessity of personal proclamation (Rom. 10:12-15)
5. The terrible consequences of rejecting the Gospel (Rom. 1:18, 2 Thess. 1:6-10)
6. The believer's missionary responsibility (Rom. 1:14-16, 10:13-15)

fail to fulfil our purpose in all honesty (1 Thess. 2:9-14).

B. The Relation of Mission and Ministry

Now, what is the relationship of *mission* and *ministry?* Let us first look at the basic non-theological meaning of the words. *Mission* comes from a Latin word meaning 'a sending off'. It connotes an assignment. Mission is a person's purpose and passion – that which makes his heart beat fast and fills his waking moments; the vision that puts sparkle in his eyes; the energy which compels him to press on when every muscle aches; the sense of calling, of commissioning, of ambassadorship, that stimulates the weary mind. And more – it is the obedience to a sovereign call even to sacrifice one's life in order to fulfil the assignment. That's mission.

Ministry is something else, coming from a Latin word for 'servant'. Ministry should be the natural result of mission, for without a sense of mission, ministry is purposeless, perfunctory. Ministry is the love flowing from the heart which has obeyed the call to mission. It is a pair of hands bandaging the wounded man left by the roadside (Luke 10:30-37). Most of all, it is the mind of Christ (Phil. 2:5), who came to minister and not to be ministered unto (Mark 10:45).

Some people fail to see the difference between mission and ministry, and so they debate which we are supposed to do. If the Great Commission ('Go ye into all the world') is mission, and the Great Commandment ('Love your neighbour') is ministry, they argue over which should have priority – 75% of one and 25% of the other? Or should both have equal emphasis?

I believe this is a harmful and erroneous dichotomy. It is like trying to compare your blood with your hands and feet. Which is more important? The answer is that your blood flows through your whole body, and is not in the same category as parts of the body. So our mission in life is the compulsion that flows through all our ministry.

Of course for theologians who don't believe that man is a lost sinner, or that the gospel of personal salvation needs to be proclaimed, there is no question: mission equals ministry, and ministry equals mission. They dismiss personal salvation as 'privatistic pietism'. Sin becomes mainly an attribute of

Rev Jeremiah Chienda, Chairman of the Evangelical Association of Malawi, has stated: 'God knows the sufferings, injustices, and troubles that are taking place, and he know that all of these are caused by the sinful nature of man. God wants to use us in concerned action for the needs of our communities . . . but we must first meet him and be prepared by him. We must receive the power from him . . . He deals with us as individuals.'[6]

Mr William Ofori-Atta, a candidate for President in Ghana's 1980 elections, is also a lay preacher and Bible teacher. His mission in life is to bring people to Christ; at the same time, as a Christian citizen, he is very much 'salt and light' in the nation. He told me just recently as I visited him in his home, 'Those of us who have found the Lord must not leave the evils of society to be solved by the children of the Devil!'

Paul reminded Titus of his personal salvation and of the great hope of the ekklesia. He also instructed him about the believer's relationship to man. Paul saw no conflict between the two relationships – the horizontal (to man) was the necessary consequence of the vertical (to God).

> When the kindness of God our Saviour and His love for mankind appeared, He saved us, not on the basis of deeds which we have done in righteousness but according to His mercy, by the washing of regeneration and renewing of the Holy Spirit, whom He poured out upon us richly through Jesus Christ our Saviour, that being justified by His grace we might become heirs according to the hope of eternal life. This is a trustworthy statement, and concerning these things I want you to speak confidently, so that those who have believed God may be careful to engage in good deeds. These things are good and profitable for men. (Titus 3:4-8)

Evangelicals have an outstanding record of meeting human need.[7] Then why do liberals accuse us of being 'heavenly minded' while neglecting 'salvation today' on the earth? I believe this is because liberals don't understand the relation of our mission and our ministry. In fact, social action (in the temporal realm) has become their mission, to the neglect of the eternal realm. When they look at evangelicals, they observe that our consuming sense of mission is centred in spiritual action (the eternal realm). Since many liberals do not believe that spiritual regeneration is essential, they cannot accept our order of priority. They hardly notice the 'good' which we minister as we go about our mission.

Concordat), but many others opposed colonial policies and evils connected with foreign trade. Bishop Patrick Kalilombe of Malawi states: 'Much of the early history of the Christian missions in Malawi concerns struggles and misunderstandings between the colonial administration and the missionaries.'[9]

'Imperialist' types tend to loom larger in the public's memory than the self-effacing types who sacrificed all they had to identify with oppressed peoples. Yet the resultant image produces reactions which affect all expatriate missionaries.[10]

Today a missionary is in the fortunate position of being divested of superior racial status and political backing, so that his message stands on its own merits.[11]

So the ekklesia has a mission – a paramount purpose which implies vision and motivation to achieve its goals. The ekklesia/ congregation commissions people who have the spiritual gifts need to carry out specific aspects of that mission (Acts 13:2,3). Those who fulfil that mission (purpose) across cultural boundaries are called missionaries.

It doesn't really matter what system the ekklesia uses to care for the work and welfare of those missionaries, as long as they fulfil their mission/purpose. The ekklesia may be able to care for and direct them through the structure of the local church. Or it may prefer to do so through the structure of its denomination, so that a denominational mission board may look after common functions on behalf of several local churches.

Or the ekklesia may channel its missionaries through another structure, a mission society, which has been set up to specialize in the work and care of missionaries. By concentrating on this specialized task, the mission society can help the local church fulfil its mission – as long as it does not become an end in itself. It must be accountable to the local church and should work in close liaison, not competition, with other structures of the ekklesia, such as denominations of like faith.

But why have *any* mission board or society to carry out the mission of the ekklesia? For one thing, the logistics of caring for cross-cultural workers in distant places require a certain amount of organization, and that requires structure.

Apart from the practical need, history has demonstrated that the ekklesia's missionary purpose is best carried out by a task force committed to that purpose. Human nature being what it is, the

We need to rediscover what I call 'aggressive evangelism'. The Christian faith is always a missionary-oriented faith. We should not let the fire of evangelism die out of our churches today. We should not get pre-occupied with what we are going to eat, what we are going to clothe ourselves with and how we are going to renovate our churches — at the expense of what is really essential, the salvation of the soul.

IV. CONCLUSION

We evangelicals would say this to men and women of liberal theological persuasion:
'We realise that you find it difficult to understand our view of the church, its mission, and its ministry. We would like you to have the same viewpoint; but if not, we ask you at least to be tolerant of us. We note a liberal ecumenical tolerance of non-Christan religions, and yet an intolerance of our Christian evangelical position.
'We politely but resolutely refuse the labels which some of you pin on us:

'(1) We are not colonialists. We follow in the tradition of the New Testament apostles. Before any of this century's colonial powers existed, the apostles preached the gospel to other peoples.
'(2) Our missionaries' primary purpose is not to change culture; but they teach the universal Word of God, which judges all cultures in God's terms.[15] Anthropologists who charge that the gospel destroys culture seem to forget that national politics and international trade bring about great cultural changes. Conversely, Christian linguists have actually helped preserve culture by saving vernacular languages from dying out.
'(3) We are not arrogant in proclaiming that Jesus Christ is the only way of salvation. He gave his life for all mankind in the greatest act of humility ever known (Phil.2:5-11). Yet he declared himself to be the unique Saviour of the world (John 14:6). As his disciples we proclaim him as Lord and Saviour in the same spirit of humility and veracity (Acts 17:22-31)[16].
'(4) We are not racially motivated. We do not believe any race is superior nor any inferior. The gospel has come to all of us from other races. Every race has within it evangelical Christians who are motivated to witness not only to their own people but to other peoples as well.
'(5) We do not ignore the socio-political bondage of man, nor are

threatening the very existence of evangelical Christianity in Africa. In the year 2000 will the vast number of Christians in Africa be Bible-oriented? Or will there be a vast number who do not yet have the light – the biblical faith?'[19]

Is the ekklesia in Africa – perhaps less than 10% of the population – prepared to respond to Christ's call for spiritual labourers? Are we prepared to look beyond our own community, beyond our own ethnic group, beyond our own nation, beyond our continent, to join hands with other members of Christ's ekklesia around the world to fulfil the Great Commission? Yes, by God's grace – as we realize the nature of the church, help to fulfil its mission and actively participate in its ministry.

NOTES

(1) John Calvin comments: 'In human transactions some procedure is always in effect, which is to be respected in the interests of public decency, and even in humanity itself. This ought especially to be observed in churches, which are best sustained when all things are under a well-ordered constitution, and which without concord become no churches at all. Therefore, if we wish to provide for the safety of the church we must attend Paul's command that "all things be done decently and in order" ' *(Institutes*, Book IV, Ch.X, Sect. 27.)

(2) W. Harold Fuller, *Mission Church Dynamics* (Pasadena, CA: William Carey Library, 1980), p.40

(3) *Ibid.* p.83

(4) Dr Rene Padilla of Argentina states: 'For the Liberation Theologians, salvation is fundamentally political liberation. They believe in sin solely as institutionalized in the structures of society. That is the Marxist approach to sin. What really matters is not whether man feels separated from God, but that he has to find his place within a history which is in the process of transformation.' (From a message at PANCLA, 1976, published in *Facing the Challenges* (Kisumu, Kenya: Evangel Publishing House, 1978), p.429)

(5) *Ibid.,* p.58

(6) Jeremiah Chienda, in *Facing the New Challenges* (Kisumu, Kenya: Evangel Publishing House, 1978), pp.347-348.

(7) W. Harold Fuller, 'Evangelicals and Community Development', in *New Horizons in World Mission*, ed. David J. Hesselgrave (Grand Rapids, MI: Baker, 1979), p. 183.

(8) Dr F.I.D. Konotey-Ahulu, in *Evangelical Times* (London, Dec. 1980), p.11

(9) A. Kalilombe, quoted by Waldron Scott in *Bring Forth Justice* (Grand Rapids, MI: Eerdmans, 1980), p.17

(10) Fuller, *op. cit.,* p.25

(11) *Ibid.,* p.24

11

Evangelism and Development

VINAY SAMUEL AND CHRIS SUGDEN

A DEFINITION

True evangelism, that brings the Gospel to the whole person, means making the Good News of Jesus Christ real to the entire person, to all people, to the community as a whole, and relating it to the whole creation. The goal is to present the Lordship of Christ so that the whole community acknowledges his Lordship.

The Gospel in the New Testament is the Good News of the Kingdom of God (Mark 1:14,15; Matt. 4:17). The Kingdom of God is a new realm of right relationships between people and nature. It is the rule of God, where God's will is done, on earth as it is in heaven (Matt. 6:10). It is the rule of God where God's righteousness (or right relationships) is established.

This Good News of the Kingdom cannot be limited to a verbal message. It can be focused in words for a particular situation, but the Good News of the Kingdom is about God's rule over every aspect of life.

JESUS IS LORD

The Gospel is good news of the Kingdom, where Jesus is Lord.

1. Jesus is now risen and Lord over the world

The distinctive message that made the early Christians different from the rest of the Jewish community out of which they came was their unshakeable belief that Jesus Christ was risen from the

2:14,15 Paul says that on the cross Christ 'disarmed the principalities and powers and made a public example of them, triumphing over them in him'. In Paul's thought these powers are supernatural powers which can be present in individuals in demon possession, but also in demonic forces behind structures in society, such as the state and the Jewish religious leadership of the time. Christ triumphed over their rebellion against God on the cross and is sovereign over them. He is continually disarming them by overcoming the injustice in society created by their rebellion. This work is not necessarily exercised only by the church. Whenever justice replaces injustice. Christ's victory over evil thus overcomes demonic spirits in persons, and also demonic forces behind social injustices. It is a victory over evil, in whichever way that evil expresses itself.

5. Jesus is Lord over all the forces and divisions which would bring enmity between groups of people

Paul writes in Ephesians 2:11-18 that Jesus unites hostile groups (in this case Jews and Gentiles) in one new humanity. He has overcome the barriers between groups of people which express their rebellion against God.

Our concern in evangelism that is holistic is, therefore, to demonstrate that Jesus is truly Lord of every aspect of people's lives, and of the whole context and situation in which people are set. It is to bring the Good News of God's Kingdom as a reality into every community.

Paul tells us how we can express Jesus' Lordship. Ephesians 2:8-10 tells us that, while we do not need good works in order to acknowledge that Christ is Lord, once we acknowledge him as Lord, we express his Lordship over us by our good works.

Our good works are the expression of the work of God's grace in our lives. God's grace is expressed not only in our faith, but also in our good works.

Jesus gave the same teaching in Matthew 5:16 – that our light must shine before men so that they may see our good works and give glory to the Father who is in heaven.

Thus our good works, in response to the real needs of people, express God's workmanship in our lives and bring glory to God. They are part of the strategy of bringing the Gospel to the whole person.

STRATEGY FOR EVANGELIZING A PEOPLE GROUP

Our first task must be to identify the real needs of the people. We must not assume what the real needs of the people are from our formulation of the Gospel. We should first of all spend time identifying the needs of the community. We should not believe the needs of the community are automatically defined, or assume that we can just speak about Jesus Christ, sin, forgiveness, salvation, and so on, and think we have communicated the Gospel. All these terms may have little relevance to people struggling with various difficulties. Terms such as 'forgiveness' and 'accepting Christ' will become tremendously meaningful later, as we identify the needs and link these up. But first, identification of the needs of those we are trying to reach is very important.

After identifying the needs, we need to educate people about one particular basic need and share our various Christian perspectives around that need. We should use that need to explain the gospel, relate the gospel to it and also enable the people to see that God addresses their fundamental need *as a community*, not merely as individuals. For we are talking about moving an entire community towards Christ.

Then, having related that, we should begin in prayer and sharing to open ourselves to God and say, 'God, this is the need of this people as a community. We want to stand together with them in this need and want you to work through this need so that your Lordship and power is beautifully demonstrated in their lives.' Begin to do that, and you will begin to see a remarkable change.

CASE STUDY FROM BURMA

The Buddhist people have traditionally been most resistant to the Gospel in Burma. But recently there has been a change. How has this happened?

There was a young man who was an immigrant into Burma. He was Chinese and, as such, had no citizen rights in Burma. He held only a tourist pass which he had to have validated each year. So he had no legal rights within that country and was therefore not only very insecure, but was also marginalized. If anybody wanted to mistreat him, he had no grounds for redress, because he had no legal basis in the country on which he could stand firmly. But despised outcast widows in the elements of pre-natal and post-natal care; they established their credentials as healers by running a small operating theatre. In this way they addressed the very serious problem of infant and child mortality. But they also addressed the problem of caste. They 'walked women through the Gospels' and showed how Jesus gave equality to women. On the basis of Jesus' authority the widows began to gain self-respect and overcome their sense of inferiority to higher castes. The Aroles addressed the problems of terror of the spirits, by showing that the villagers had no need to fear some days as inauspicious for medical operations; the God of the Bible was Lord of every day.

As a result of their work, the villagers have now accepted Jesus as their god. He has replaced their local village deities and they now worship him in the fully biblical presentation of Jesus, as incarnate Son of God, who lived, died, rose again and is returning to reign.

These case studies show that holistic involvement is vitally necessary from the very beginning of our relationship with a community of people. A clear space must be made for development activity and involvement in the total life of the people. Only if this is done will the impact of the Gospel beyond the initial stages of its presentation be holistic. We cannot undermine the holism of the Gospel by expecting holism to come later.

Through expressing a Christian value system, in the way we identify the real needs of the community and work to meet those needs by God's power, we are painting a portrait of Jesus. We are showing the sort of things Jesus identifies as real needs; we are showing what sort of things he cares about; we are showing how he helps. The portrait is best painted by a group of Christians. For Jesus' Lordship and victory is demonstrated as barriers are broken down between previously separated groups – Jews and Gentiles, men and women. Thus the full dimensions of the portrait cannot be painted by an individual alone, through words alone. We may have to paint the full portrait before we give it its title. Jesus waited till he had painted his own full portrait, and shown the cost of discipleship, before he allowed people to name his name as Christ, the Son of God. In the same way, people may have their own distorted ideas about who Jesus is. We need therefore to paint a true and authentic portrait of him through our involvement with them before we name his name.

problems of other people – despair, loneliness, divorces, drug addiction, poverty.

The second orientation is a transformation orientation. God's grace comes into the situation of a community of people and totally transforms every aspect of it. He heard the cries of migrant labourers in Egypt, subject to ruthless exploitation of their labour and a forced birth control policy, and delivered them totally to possess a land of their own where they might worship God. He heard the cries of the women, the sick, the children, widows, and the lepers in the first century, and totally transformed the situation by creating a series of new communities of forgiveness, equality and sharing.

Jesus and Paul shared the Good News with people in the expectation that their whole world view, sense of self-worth and relationships with others would be totally transformed. This meant changes for the poor – and also for the rich who had to forego preferential treatment, pay their labourers just wages and repay those whom they had defrauded, if they wanted to join. The purpose of transformation is not relief only, but that people may engage in good works (Eph.4:23) – in other words service to bring social transformation.

It is our contention that much evangelistic activity, especially in mass evangelism, continues to provide a relief perspective as the basic Christian perspective on life. Therefore evangelicals respond to relief appeals enthusiastically and find appeals to development to be suspect because they are seen as man's efforts.

It is therefore essential that first we examine our evangelistic activity in proclamation, mass evangelism, and the use of radio and TV media to see what perspective it promotes on life in general. Secondly, we must modify it to promote a holistic perspective (by which we mean a perspective that integrates transformation *and* relief). Can this be done without an integration of evangelistic activities with development for social transformation? It is our contention that a development perspective is of critical importance to all evangelistic activity, especially in the Two Thirds world.

IMPLICATIONS

The implications are as follows. While we may distinguish between social service and social action, it is our contention that authentic

12

Resources for New Frontier Missions

TEO J. V.D. WEELE

INTRODUCTION

Three streams of visionaries are calling for the Church's attention. Some, looking beyond the confines of their culture and its time-bound concepts, see a world lost without Christ. Reaching thousands of these 'hidden' or 'unreached' peoples seems an attainable goal.

Other visionaries see the need for renewal of the Church and its mission in its local setting.

A third stream of visionaries has seen the spectre of unparalleled human misery. They foresee that things will become much worse. The dehumanization, the degradation, the agony, the hell-here-on-earth at times can pale whatever other priorities one has. What then is the evangelical answer?

Each stream wants its vision to be translated into action, theology translated into a budget. They each pull at the Church. I believe that the crucial issue is: 'Are we pulling apart, or pulling together?'

THE NEED FOR A THEOLOGY OF RESOURCES

Dr Paul Hieber states: 'We need a theology of power and resources'.[1]

(1) How do we translate our theological convictions into action? What processes are there to consider? Such a theology could help

decided against certain aspects of computerization in order to create jobs.

f) The 'church/para-church' tension has appreciable affects in our personal and corporate decision-making. I heard in Bangkok of a para-church leader who was sent to 'select the best evangelical national and offer him twice the salary he is earning at present'. The local church is unable to move away from neighbourhood problems and unresponsiveness. I have seen how unwise missions recruiting depleted a local church of key people. In their eagerness to harvest, they 'ripped out the roots' of a church. On the other hand mission leaders weep when they see unused talent wasting away in shoddily-run churches; and believers unwilling to celebrate the principle of tithing, thus allowing capable pastors or evangelists to suffer. What do you do then, when a para-church agency is eager, pioneering and waiting?

g) The stress on *verbal* proclamation through witnessing, preaching, the printed page, radio, TV and video is evident everywhere.

But do people change? There seems to be a 'spiritual energy crisis'. Burned-out activists are everywhere. Are we doing something wrong? I hear European young people saying: 'If this is all that the ministry can offer, tired, neurotic, uptight Christian workers, then I'd rather not get involved . . .' Our inability to choose, to set priorities; our attempts to do everything, to enter any open door, is hurting new recruiting.

The same Holy Spirit who helped Paul to take a decision and to choose is there to lead us. Dr Octavianus' paper on 'Divine Resources' (pp.00-00) gives some indication of how silence, reflection and worship is needed in order for us to hear the whisper of the Dove, prompting us and pointing the way.

WHICH THEOLOGY OF RESOURCES DO WE HAVE?

A theology of resources consists of at least three elements: the foundation; the people involved; and the methods used by God.

(1) **On what foundations do we build?**

We should consider at least three types of resources: *spiritual*, *human* and *material*. We often give an ideal picture of the right

'The Lord is very patient with you, because it is not his will for any to be lost, but for all to come to repentance . . .'

In Europe, we face more and more the need to restate the awesome plight of those outside of Christ. Universalism is having a deep effect upon the evangelical movement. The OMF felt it necessary to research the issue and to publish a special book called *God, it's not fair*. The heart of God is crying for those who are living and dying without Christ. He doesn't want any one to be lost. I have discovered that from time to time I was very orthodox in my mind, but liberal in my heart. Increasingly I am becoming aware of the pain which God must suffer as he faces a world which refuses to believe. Modern research highlights for us the scope of this tragedy as we think of the many people groups who have never had a decent chance to hear the Gospel in a meaningful way.

GOD'S METHOD, THE CHURCH

(1) **The renewed church**

God has chosen to work through people who, under the leadership of Jesus Christ, together form one body. With Jesus Christ as foundation, we must be careful what we are building on that foundation. History proves that all too often churches renewed by the Holy Spirit have turned into monuments of human endeavour. Not all chronologically old churches *are* old. Some have a built-in renewal tradition. On the other hand I know some charismatic churches who, after ten years of existence, have 'seen it all' and are tired and disappointed. Renewal is possible, renewal is needed.

Old churches need the 'Sarah-solution'; they need faith. They should not just be renewed, but should believe that through faith they can have children in their 'old age'. God's heart cries for new churches. 'Sarah' should hear and respond in faith.

(2) **Restoration**

Renewal might be a correction of some foundational problems. Social issues and mission can be used as cosmetics to improve the church's image. The 'hidden peoples' approach so fervently and

N.I.M. —I

The answer is one of spiritual management.

I would like to present the outlines of two biblical models plus some practical applications to show how we could go on in the development and sharing of resources.

TWO BIBLICAL MODELS IN THE USE OF RESOURCES

(1) **Psalm 23**

As a pastoral counsellor and as a consultant to local churches I have found Psalm 23 to be an excellent guide for both personal and organizational development.

Between 'The Lord is my Shepherd' and the final phrase 'I will dwell in the house of the Lord', there is quite a path. How do you get there? Lately I have felt more and more the need to start my questioning with the basic question: 'What does God want? How does he feel?'

God *wants* to be a Shepherd for us. His heart cry goes out to the lost, wounded sheep. To fulfil his plan, he calls 'under-shepherds', through whom he works out his plan. It is amazing how little the office of the shepherd has been stressed in missions. Church-planting apostles in the New Testament did give evidence of shepherding: watching the flock. How will a national pastor learn to be a shepherd without a model? Naturally an expatriate has severe limitations, but only in the cultural expressions of his role. The whole management boom in evangelical circles should carefully look at what happened in mainline churches, as given in an analysis by Dr Richard Hutcheson. 'The managerial revolution may have been one of the reasons for decline.'[3]. Shepherds as managers are in the first place people, who know the heart of God and who know the heart of their people.

Authority without accountability becomes dictatorship. Shepherds must be sheep as well. Again I believe this to be for most a spiritual matter: can we give 'pride of place' to others, can we yield? Through heart relationships between workers in God's Kingdom, through a commitment to each other which is rooted in the heart of God, we see a new unity across cultures and generation gaps. The problem is that organizations can more easily maintain organizational formal ties than maintain heart relationships.

need attention. The man with one talent was rebuked: 'You could have given your talent to the bankers.' In the management of spiritual, human and material resources, we do find situations where we are baffled. Perhaps we should have known what to do, but we don't. The cry is then: 'Where are the evangelical bankers, who know what to do?' Obviously, Matt. 25 is a call for leadership.

The second theme in this parable, next to 'obedience', is 'community': 'You are not alone, others have gifts; work together.' The shepherd-manager, using heart relations as a key and the community concept in leadership, could give us answers with regard to resource-sharing between different groups. Third World missions do need resources. Yet a Western style of accountability is often felt as being 'over-lording'. But how can those who have, share with those who don't have? A trust relationship between leaders across the globe, founded on spiritual encounters on a prolonged basis, could show a way out.

CONCLUSION

I would hope that new ways can be found to:

(1) Bridge the gap between cultures and traditions through spiritual teams, which can function as catalysts in the different regions of the world. Shepherd/teachers are especially needed in order to foster person-to-person heart relationships which will provide the linkage in the Body of Christ.

(2) Make creative links. The great variety of 'all God's people' across the globe flocks together in many forms. Intercultural catalyst teams could attempt to provide linkage between compatible groups. This could enhance the partnership which Larry Keyes proposed in 'The Last Age of Missions'. In mutual recognition and trust a great variety of forms of resource-sharing might take place.

(3) Promote resource-sharing — which will happen if one keeps in mind in the following diagram:

   1. The right order of sharing; first spiritual, then people, then material;

of knowledge and experience. They could also aid older missions in their renewal programmes. They would serve only when invited, with an authority which was spiritual and recognition of their competence based on their past record. Such people could be the backbone of a growing movement of international evangelical cooperation.

The strong foundation of spirituality for such a global interlocking project has been most forcefully stated by Dr Bruce Nicholls.

We cannot hope to develop a global inter-locking project whose goal is both the renewal and the growth of the Church without engaging in a conflict with the ruler of this world.

NOTES

(1) A.F. Glasser, ed., *Crucial dimensions in world evangelization* (Pasadena: W. Carey Lib., 1976), p.85
(2) L. Keyes, *The Last Age of Missions*, p.84
(3) *International Bulletin of Missions Research* Vol.7 no.2 (April, 1983), p.73

THE HOLY SPIRIT AS THE AGENT OF GOD'S POWER

When the Lord Jesus Christ, before his ascension to the Father, charged his disciples with the Great Commission, he also gave them the promise of the Holy Spirit as the agent of the divine power to execute his commission to the ends of the earth. We read in Acts 1:8:

> But ye shall receive power, after that the Holy Ghost is come upon you: and ye shall be witnesses unto me both in Jerusalem, and in all Judea, and in Samaria, and unto the uttermost part of the earth.

Clearly we see here God's plan for the thrust of the Gospel through the Holy Spirit: through his power, by his witnesses, and to the ends of the earth.

In 1967 our Bible College experienced the visitation of the Holy Spirit. For two whole months academic work came to a standstill. Classes were cancelled as the whole student body prayed together with the staff, and we experienced the convicting power of the Holy Spirit and his cleansing from sin and from occult bondages. The Holy Spirit then mightily anointed the teams going forth throughout all of Indonesia, from Sabang, North Sumatra, in the western part of Indonesia, to the Moluccas in the eastern part, and from Sangir Talaud, in the northern part, to Timor, in the southern part. The Gospel teams, consisting of two, three or five members each, one hundred in total (both staff and students), were used by the Lord to bring the fire of the Holy Spirit everywhere they went. Since that time the Lord has used our fellowship in a unique ministry in many places, to deliver people from occult bondages and from demon possession. Such a ministry is especially relevant in Indonesia today, where the culture is still strongly influenced by animism. Even in many churches of our country so-called Christians depend on fetishes, charms and folk medicine.

In this modern space age, it is very easy to substitute modern technology and methodology for the 'grace and power' orientation of the New Testament. Michael Griffiths, in his book *Shaking the Sleeping Beauty*, states:

> As regards the ends of missions and church building we have become programme-oriented instead of goal-oriented; so also in

must depend on God's resources, gifts and power. They must take time to visit on the Lord so to ascertain his will and activate his power. We have been warned by the example of those from the Third World, who went to Europe for graduate work, but diverted from their pure evangelical faith and theology and are now no longer useful for the Lord here in Asia. They have lost the strength that comes from prayer and the anointing he gives, when we wait upon him.

OCCASION TWO: CROSS-CULTURAL MISSION. ACTS 8:1-25; 26-40.

Through the persecution that arose after the death of Stephen the Holy Spirit moved some of the witnesses from the mono-cultural situation in Jerusalem into cross-cultural situations of missionary outreach. In this way, Philip came to Samaria and began to preach Christ to the despised Samaritans. His preaching was accompanied by mighty works of deliverance from powers of darkness, and by miracles of healing. In the midst of busy days of evangelism in Samaria, the voice of the Lord told him to go to the south and contact the Ethiopian eunuch on the road to Gaza. Missionary calls always start with God commanding us to 'go and make disciples of all nations'. Indeed Philip proved himself as a cross-cultural missionary, both by his ministry in Samaria and when he led the Ethiopian eunuch to saving faith in Christ.

At present, the cross-cultural count of our fellowship stands as follows: 180 members; 135 serving as home-missionaries, six serving abroad (2 in Surinam, 2 in India, 1 in Bangladesh and 1 in Nepal); 2 more couples and 3 singles waiting for their visa to Pakistan, Bangladesh and Gambia: 39 missionaries from other countries, such as Germany, Holland, Norway, Finland, Australia, New Zealand, USA, Japan and Korea who have joined the Indonesian Missionary Fellowship.

OCCASION THREE: APOSTOLIC MINISTRIES. ACTS 9:1-19.

Saul, the well-educated Pharisee and member of the Sanhedrin, persecutor of Christians and by-stander at the death of Stephen, met with the Lord Jesus on the road to Damascus and experienced a dramatic conversion. Healed and filled with the Holy Spirit receptive listeners. Hearing about these things, and the openness of the Serawai people to the gospel, I went with some of the students from the Bible Institute to South Sumatra in 1964. Arriving in the Serawai area, we also found many religious leaders open to the gospel and hungry for God's word. They received the Lord, were baptized and became themselves pioneers of the gospel in Serawai, bringing into existence the Serawai Church which now numbers some 3500 members.

OCCASION FIVE: PLANTING OF THE ANTIOCH CHURCH THROUGH LAY-MEN. ACTS 11:19-26.

Because of the persecution in Jerusalem, believers from there went everywhere and testified for the Lord Jesus Christ. In the founding of the Antioch church, the Holy Spirit clearly directed *non-apostles* to start this work among Jews and Greeks. Ever since, the Holy Spirit has been pleased to use Spirit-filled, dedicated lay-men to share the glorious gospel with those who have never heard it, and to start churches in different levels of various societies and cultures, then and now.

Through the evangelistic crusades of our fellowship many lay people have come into a living relationship with the Lord Jesus Christ. Through seminars on evangelism they then learn how to become witnesses for him. Everywhere they go, they witness for the Lord: in their homes in their neighbourhood, and at their places of work. They start prayer groups. They have taken an interest in our mission work. At present, some 340 prayer groups have sprung up as a direct result of our evangelistic crusades, and these groups are connected with our fellowship.

We also reach many lay people through our Annual Convention. For 19 years believers from all over Indonesia have gathered in Batu for six days of revival and deeper life meetings. The number of people attending has steadily risen to nearly 3000!

The Lord has also used students from our Bible Institute to establish churches with lay people in the areas surrounding Batu. One example is the birth of the Javanese church in Pujon. When our students went there for evangelism, they met an illiterate woman to whom they witnessed concerning the death and resurrection of Christ. They also gave her a Bible, which she took home to her husband. He also became a believer. Both of them

Prayer is the most vital element in our lives, individually and as a group. Daily we bring our needs to the Lord. Once a month, the whole fellowship gathers for prayer, students included; this besides the daily morning 'chapels'. We have weekly fellowship prayer meetings for staff, and further meetings once a month. In answer to prayer, the Lord often moves in the hearts of men and women who have been reached through our evangelistic crusades or who are in our prayer groups, or who have been helped through personal counselling, to contribute to the fellowship with financial means. Indeed, in our twenty years of existence the Indonesian Missionary Fellowship can truly say that the Lord has met all our needs, out of the resources of his power and his grace.

OCCASION SEVEN: LIVING TOGETHER. ACTS 13:1, 2:44a.

Our members come from eleven different nations, and from such varied cultural, racial and educational backgrounds truly learn, through the work of the Cross of Christ in our lives, how to worship, serve and live together. We try to avoid little 'islands' in our fellowship, where Germans meet only with the Germans, or Norwegians with Norwegians, or Bataks with Bataks, or Timorese with Timorese; members of different backgrounds are put into living and working relationships with each other.

We all learn to know and accept one another in our different lifestyles and ways. When new missionaries come from abroad, they are given a period for adjustment, a two-year 'probationary time', just the same as the new fellowship members from within our country. (See page 00.)

OCCASION EIGHT: MINISTERING TOGETHER.
ACTS 15:22-35;20:4; 18:26.

There are many examples in the book of Acts of how the Lord's people ministered together in various ways. There is the Aquila-Priscilla team in Acts 18:26. There is Paul's team, in Acts 20:4, men who went with him, from various backgrounds, to minister with him and learn from him.

Within our mission we agree that our integration must be manifested in our work together as one body. The positions of

Commission, by penetrating unreached areas and groups of people with the Gospel, and equipping believers for their witness.

BIBLIOGRAPHY

Michael Griffiths, *Shaking the Sleeping Beauty* (Leicester: IVP, 1980)
George Peters, *A Theology of Church Growth* (Grand Rapids, Michigan: Zondervan, 1981)
Waldron Scott, 'The Task Before Us', in J. Douglas, ed., *Let the Earth Hear His Voice* (Minneapolis, Minn: Worldwide Publications), pp. 18-21
Philip Teng, in *Christ Seeks Asia*, ed. Stanley Mooneyham (Hong Kong: The Rock House Publishers), pp. 56-57
The Holy Bible, King James Edition.
Petrus Octavianus, 'Integration', unpublished paper (1980, Batu Malang, Indonesia).

(a) *'Reach' should mean 'incorporate'*

Some will question however, why – if we are simply trying to give everyone a valid opportunity to accept Christ – it is necessary to emphasize the presence or absence of the church (as does our definition of an unreached people). In my thinking, and in the thinking of all those who employ this criterion, there is no such thing as 'a valid opportunity to accept Christ' apart from the indigenous presence of his church. Don't misunderstand me! What I am saying is rather technical. I agree that conceivably a person can accept Christ apart from a church in his context. But normally this is not the way people become Christians, and even if they do, it is not ideal. People do not simply turn on a switch in their hearts or minds in some kind of direct relationship to God and then proceed to grow spontaneously in their new faith. Normally, they need to be incorporated into his fellowship, into his Church. That is the reason why the trend has been for the various definitions of unreached peoples to take into account the presence or absence of an indigenous church.

(b) *Reaching Groups is Faster*

Apart from the fact that it is more biblical to emphasize the salvation of peoples, not individuals only, it is also true that it is easier to give individuals a valid opportunity to accept Christ if you can get to them within their community, on their own wavelength, through a fellowship of believers that they can understand and by whom they will be understood. That strategy is both a better *and* a faster way to reach people. Some today may think it is more efficient to evangelize the world by spraying the globe with electromagnetic radiation in the form of radio or television. Such efforts are all to the good. But evangelizing at arm's length by radio is not the same as reaching people on their own personal wavelength and within their own culture. Someone once said to me, 'It's possible today by satellite to project a message into every home in the world.' And I answered, 'What language are you going to use? Muslims alone speak 580 different languages.' He paused, as he should have, because we are not speaking of mass communication when we evangelize. Jesus was not content with merely a public ministry. He poured most of his energy into one people group, and became himself a part of that group. Ultimately we are dealing with very, very specific communication to the heart,

(e) *Pseudo-unreached Groups*

What are unreached peoples? There are some people groups which seem to be unreached, but really aren't. Let us say that among the refugees from Southeast Asia in the United States today there are 1000 members of a certain tribal group who now live in Philadelphia. Among them there is not one Christian. Are these people an unreached people? Who knows, maybe in New York City there are 100,000 more from the same tribe. The subgroup in New York may have strong, fast growing churches and well educated pastors, and the Bible may be in their language. In that event, it would be folly to treat the Philadelphia people group as though it were an unreached people, and for an ordinary American to try to learn their language and translate the Bible into their tongue if someone, somewhere else, had already done this. A group of people among whom there is no church or Christians is not an unreached people if the same group elsewhere is reached.

(f) *Pseudo-reached Groups*

You can also go wrong in the opposite direction. That is, a people may be 'pseudo-reached' even though they have a church. There is such a thing as a dead church; indeed, deadness and liveness are the essence of our subject here. A pseudo-reached group of this sort may have some missionaries, and some Christians, but it lacks a vital church. The church present in that culture is unable to reach out and evangelize the people of the culture because the church itself needs to be evangelized. 'Unreachedness' is thus not defined on the basis of whether there are any Christians or not, or whether there are any missionaries working among them or not. It is defined on the basis of whether or not in that culture there is a viable, culturally relevant, witnessing church movement.

(g) *People Distinctives: Cultural or Genetic?*

Finally, it is not always easy to determine clearly one's own 'people group'. There are some people who believe that in determining people groups we should consider only ethno-linguistic distinctions. I will not argue with them, but I do think that the label 'ethno-linguistic' combines in one phrase itself both genetic and cultural factors. If, therefore, we are going to combine genetic and cultural factors in our descriptions of people, why not admit it from the picture in Gen. 26:4, the same happens. But, as we have seen, when Jacob comes into the picture in Gen. 28:14, *mishpaha* is used again (*ethne* in the Septuagint). I cannot detect any contextual reason why there is that shifting back and forth unless, in actual fact, these are synonymous terms, and indeed they are in part. There are 60 *mishpaha* that went into the promised land; these are smaller groups.

But several of these *mishpaha* belonged to single tribes since there were only twelve tribes. One of these *mishpaha* happened to be a tribe all by itself. Thus a small *goyim* is sometimes called a *mishpaha*. (Here I am drawing on an unpublished paper by Richard Showalter.)

(a) *Megapeoples, Macropeoples, Minipeoples and Micropeoples.*

Even in English, when you speak of the Chinese people you refer to a billion people who represent many, many peoples in terms of missionary strategy. In groping for a terminology to define strategic units more precisely, I have tried to press into duty the following unpronounceable series of words. If, for example, we refer to the Han Chinese, we are speaking about only the 'Chinese-ish' citizens of China. The tribal peoples of China would not be included in this category. But the specifically Han peoples include not only those in China, but also the Han peoples outside of China. Thus, politics and political boundaries are of lesser significance in this study. More important is what we could call 'peoplehood' – a sense of belonging to each other. The Han Chinese, then, could be considered a 'megapeople' – which is my largest category of definition of peoples. (Note: There are small megapeoples, too, such as small tribes unrelated to any other.) Likewise, we may speak of a Hindu megapeople including all those for whom the primary orientation of their lives has come from the impress of Hinduism. But the large megapeoples have significant subdivisions.

Thus, we may proceed to notice that within the massive megapeople called the Han Chinese there are 'macropeoples' – smaller groups such as all those who are native speakers of Mandarin. I have heard that in China only 14% of the population speaks Mandarin in the home. Certainly many more understand Mandarin, since it is the official language of the country, but at home many who understand Mandarin may usually speak Shanghaiese, or Fukien, or Minnan, or Hakka, or Swatow or Cantonese, and so on. Cantonese speakers, for example, make up relationship, there may be avenues of communication that are superior to all others. Nonetheless I think that what we are really trying to do when we evangelize is to choose that avenue that will maximize the impact and acceptability of our message. It seems to me logical to assume that we are all trying to find that one maximally approachable group for any given individual. We can then say that for every person in the world there is only one people-oriented approach that, to the best of our knowledge, is the best way to teach that particular person. That way no one will be counted twice. Of course we might find out that our guesses were wrong, and then we would have to reclassify that person.

The point is that to do effective evangelism, we must ordinarily approach individuals with full recognition of their peoplehood and deal with them in the group where they can best be approached. We may therefore assume that everybody in the world is in only one group, and we can then count up the groups that result without counting anyone twice. In doing things in this way I have arrived, along with the advice of many people, at about 16,750 groups that can be called 'unreached' by the definition given here.

How Many Peoples are there?

But is the number 16,750 at all exact? We have listed 5,000 tribal, 4,000 Muslim, 3,000 Hindu, 2,000 Han Chinese and 1,000 Buddhist groups. These are clearly round numbers. In each case those three zeros are supposed to announce to everyone that these are guesses – careful, but guesses nevertheless. At this hour of history it is deplorable that no one can do better than guess. This is what MARC does. This is what the different research agencies on our campus are doing. Everyone is guessing. We are all pleading for help. And every time we guess we are constantly refining our grasp of what the task really is. Thus, when it comes to the total number of unreached peoples, I think we have to realize that once we settle in our minds that everybody belongs in only one group – which for that person is the most reachable context – then we can count the groups without counting anyone twice. Some groups are already reached (about 6,550) and some (16,750) are unreached, within a rough total of 23,300.

Somebody may remonstrate, 'But David Barrett says there are only 8,990 people groups, not 23,300.' (By the way, his book is a truly monumental study.) True, his book speaks of some 8,990 the country of Nigeria or Peruvian Amazonia, where there is a large number of different tribal groups. The so-called 'tribals' are often basically refugee populations. Constant fear of all other groups, and an imprisoned situation, are typical of tribal peoples. This trait, even if it were a common denominator, is too tenuous to make the tribal category into a cultural bloc. The 'tribals' of the world are a far bigger task than if they were a single megapeople.

Four thousand of the world's unreached peoples are in the Muslim sphere. Here we find a massive megapeople scattered all over the world, but nevertheless also concentrated in a number of places. We tend to think of the Middle East when we think of Muslims. Yet the Middle East is the smallest part of the Muslim world today. Only 7% of Muslims speak Arabic. We find larger concentrations of Muslims both east and west of Arabia, and they speak 580 major different languages. Note that although, like the 'tribals', they speak many different languages, the evangelistically significant unifying factor of Islam makes the huge Muslim category a megapeople, not just a large category like the tribal group.

Three thousand are Hindu groups, mainly concentrated in India. But again Hindus are scattered all over the world. For example, in places like Trinidad and Guyana in the Caribbean, or Fiji in the South Pacific, people with Hindu orientation constitute the majority of the population.

Two thousand are part of the Chinese megapeople. Although these peoples are perhaps a bit more concentrated than any other group, nevertheless they can be found in 61 different countries of the world.

About 1,000 are Buddhists, in a primary sense; and for vast millions of Chinese and Japanese, Buddhism is certainly a secondary factor. The heartland of Buddhism is no longer the India in which it was born but Burma, Thailand and Cambodia, for example, where its missionary influence has been more virile.

Highly significant to Americans is the fact that from each of these five major groups there are thousands upon thousands of individuals in the United States. Of course not all of the specific peoples within these larger megapeoples are represented in the United States, but many of them are, especially the reached peoples. One result of migration in the modern world is simply that we can no longer make any valid home/foreign distinctions. Once we see the world as 23,000 or so unimax peoples, it no longer you must go to Munich, Germany. Do you see what I mean? *Geography* is not as important as *peoples*. Once that is clear, the question of where they are is a very exciting one. It is very significant to consider what can happen in Munich, Germany, once we focus on peoples instead of countries.

3. UNREACHED PEOPLES: WHY?

Finally, what about the 'why'? This is the question that energizes me the most. These other questions of 'what' and 'where' I would call simply technical questions. But 'why' this subject is important is the mandate of the Gospel itself. Yet it is more than that.

I think we are in the third and final era of mission history. To speak only of the Protestant tradition, the 'first era' missionaries went out to the coastlands of the world, and after a number of years the work became somewhat stagnated. People genuinely did not believe it was useful or safe to go inland. Finally a few missionaries broke through the resistance to opening new inland fields. As a result, a whole new wave of awareness engulfed the Protestant world. All the mission agencies had assumed it was impossible to go inland until Hudson Taylor and his followers actually did it. Then, gradually, after about twenty-five years of respectful watching and waiting, the older mission boards in England and America rapidly retooled, motivated to a great extent by the impact of Moody and the rising demands of the Student Volunteer Movement. And a new rush of recruits went out to these new inland frontiers. The development was epitomized by the 1910 Edinburgh Conference, which made as its focal point the unreached areas of the world.

Nevertheless, at the very end of this second 'Student Volunteer' era, some of the younger missionaries once more began to tinker around and broke through to still another reality, which in the earlier stages was too small to be bothered with. In an earlier paper I have mentioned the whole sequence: Eliot, Nomenson, Keysser, Gutmann; then Pickett, and − preeminently for the English speaking world − McGavran and Townsend. Cameron Townsend as a colporteur for the American Bible Society in Guatemala noticed that the Indians were considered almost wallflowers, part of the environment. Everyone assumed that eventually they would learn connection to the vast bulk of Pakistanis, even though their language is more or less the same. It is absolutely folly to assume that the job is done because among certain peoples we have gotten in and made our missiological breakthrough. How foolish to assume we can now wash our hands and go home without even communicating a sense of external mission to our mission field churches!

The people back home can't easily understand this complexity. We can project the countries of the world on the screen, and they will recognize them. What we need to do now is to project on that screen the peoples of the world. On the map of Africa we would have to show that 800 of the people groups are split into two or perhaps three pieces by a political boundary.

Oh, if it were possible for people to realize how nearly within our grasp it is to evangelize the unreached peoples of the world, it would be a revolution of new hope for people all across this country! The reason our mission boards are not receiving the candidates and the funds that they need is that people in the pew have lost hope. If 30,000 missionaries are going to retire in the next decade and, as somebody has guessed, only 5,000 are going to replace them, then the present level of giving and going needs to be multiplied many times over. Research is necessary on those statistics as well if we are to turn this situation around and be the blessing to all the families of the earth which God expects us to be simply because he has so greatly blessed us. But we need to communicate hope to people. We need to tell them that 16,750 people groups is not very many after all. Do you know, I don't care if it's 10,000 or 20,000 or what the number is, but it's a finite number. And whatever the number you come up with, just divide it into the number of dedicated evangelicals on the face of the earth today (258,000,000). You'll get at least 10,000 Bible-believing, committed believers who are ready, if awakened, to reach out to each one of these people groups – 10,000 per group.

Let me ask you, is that an unrealistic goal for the year 2000? Every week there are 1,000 new churches in Africa and Asia alone. But all these churches are new churches where there are already churches. All we need is to found 1,000 per year within these untouched groups and we'll be through with this initial job of penetrating the remaining frontiers by the year 2000. I'm not going to tamper with your eschatology, but at least we ought to try to do this. That's *my* eschatology. We ought at least to try to do what is plain in Scripture, what we are expected to do in terms of the blessings we have received!

associated in their minds with abhorrent military overtones. They are used in this paper to describe preparation for judicious action. Our concern will be to plan for responsible stewardship of resources for declaring a gospel of grace and forgiveness. The terms are not used here for their military ring, or in a spirit of triumphalism. I gladly recognize our Master's words: 'Without me you can do nothing.' On the other hand, I am thankful that scriptural realism does not require us to do nothing. The question I seek to set before us is simply one of discerning and following the mind of the directive Holy Spirit. What is desired is the active obedience that will find the fruitfulness of God's choice that his Church should bear fruit abundantly and be built among all peoples to his glory.

In short, then, the term strategy is used here as a synonym for prayerful attempts to discover and do God's will. The fact is that many people engage in strategic planning without realizing it. They may do so in prayer. They pray their hopes into practical steps. Fine! Their dependence on the Spirit and their planning might be more effective if they were to look at them and rework them more formally by writing them down and holding themselves accountable by comparing the outcomes of their ministry to their expectations. Goals are really one way of making statements of faith, whether they are made in prayer or on paper. Those who make their statement of expectations to God in prayer do not proceed without any planning. We should work out a strategy and do planning as our concrete effort to 'redeem the time' in evil days. This is not contrary to the biblical model, nor to the day-to-day experience of most people. God has made us stewards of the riches he has given us, of time, energy and gifted people. All these are limited. Strategy is one part of the effort to invest these talents for Christ, rather than to bury them in a napkin of aimlessness. We attempt to carry on his business gainfully in this way.

BIBLICAL EXAMPLES

Hints in the biblical record of the life of the Apostle Paul before his conversion tell us of a man given to preparing elaborate plans to fulfil his aim of eradicating the children of 'the Way'. Character traits were firmly established whereby he had the means of accomplishing a specific purpose clear in his own mind, and then carrying it through in his attempt to reach the goals he had set possible in partnership with the Holy Spirit. Apart from this kind of scriptural groundwork, it appears totally arrogant for anyone to describe strategies for reaching all the world's peoples. When God has spoken in this way, and such clear examples are before us for our learning, such an effort is a sign rather of submissive obedience in following the leading of the Holy Spirit. We need to search out the ways in which God wants to deepen our commitment to involvement in world evangelization.

One other common misunderstanding needs to be cleared up. When we plan, we are not predetermining the future, but attempting to modify it for the better and to see and follow God's sovereignty. We are not usurping but submitting to his guidance toward greater fruitfulness. The God who planned redemption before the ages were founded seeks those who will worship him by tracing and following his ways. The Holy Spirit did not hinder Paul's party from going to the province of Asia (Bithynia, Acts 16:6,7) until they attempted actual travel.

These principles seem so simple, but reading the situation to form a framework to guide us, and setting goals within that framework, are powerful tools for improving ministry. They are also more frequently neglected than used.

STRATEGIC AND PLANNING LEVELS

Strategy and planning can be done at many levels. The temptation is to attempt a sweeping situational analysis of the whole world. I want to resist that and pick out, in what may seem a highly arbitrary fashion, two major trends, and then move toward my major point, that the most important strategy we can have is a strategy developed for the particular case of an unreached group of people. Too many attempt to apply a favourite method or set of practices to all situations. I would like to argue that we need to define a group, and from the particular needs and circumstances of that group listen to God's Spirit until we can apply spiritual ministry to those needs in a fashion that will be recognized by them as good news. I will also incidentally consider some aspects of the way mission has been carried out until now.

the world, gospel missionaries have been acutely conscious of peoples and cultures. It is likely that the modern science of anthropology owes as much to the work of missionaries as to the fieldwork of scientists. Indeed, for one period of history European social scientists depended far more on facts and descriptions from missionaries than on their own fieldwork. With numerous dictionaries to his credit, William Carey could hardly be accused of a lack of people consciousness. The great wave of faith missions extending around the world to focus on ethnic groups and tribal languages for a while almost paralleled the selfishness inherent in the anthropologist's undue pride in 'my tribe'. As a matter of practice, mission agencies instinctively selected peoples and planted churches among them.

At time the church has taken other units as a focus for thought and action. It has not worked. The mistaken direction taken when, for example, the modern nation-state was used as the basis of analysis caused tremendous loss of momentum. The concept of people groups is the most appropriate base for strategy and planning.

2. World-Class Cities

The development of world-class cities is important for strategic reasons, far weightier than merely that they will contain in the immediate future such a high proportion of humankind. Cities have always had strategic importance. As has been emphasized in modern missiological writing, they are important biblically, and formed the framework of the strategy of the Apostle Paul as he sought to unite the peoples and fill the world with the Church of Christ. They *are* important because they group together so many people, many of whom are open to the gospel for a short 'window' in time. More than half the population of whole continents is located in cities. But they have also always been important as centres of influence on all of life. Riches, political power, productive capability, communications capacity, cultural development and preservation – all these centre in cities and are important to the spread of the gospel.

The trend toward internationalization of cities is evidence that God is proceeding to tie the world together in ways that we have not formerly dreamed possible. Each of the world-class cities is important to us because of the flow of peoples in and out of them.

dependent on literacy, yet we virtually require people to become literate before they can become disciples. In the Old Testament we have the slimmest basis to warrant this kind of notion: a king of Israel was required to make and keep his own copy of the law (Torah). This has led us to construct a theology of written scriptures.

I do not intend to confront the theologian with the idea that God did not mean to perpetuate and preserve his message through the ages by written scriptures. These guarantee a degree of permanence which is impossible when tradition is passed on by word of mouth based on memory. But we do need to rethink the question of what is translation. To what medium should the Scriptures be translated? We prepare pastors and evangelists to depend on communication skills found only in a literate tradition. This has meant that older and wiser leadership has often been set aside, displaced by younger people who are trained in the communication skills dependent on literacy. Herb Klem has challenged us to rethink this whole approach.

On conservative estimates, as much as 70 per cent of the world may not be functionally literate. While 99 per cent of the world's people have the Bible printed in their language, at least 50 per cent of them are illiterate. The richness and variety of non-literate traditions ought to be permeated with attempts to communicate apart from writing. Some examples might be found in the fields of ethnomusicology and drama. Certainly the use of the 'kirtan' – epic poetry sung at the great religious fairs in India – would be a case in point.

While I am on the subject, there is a further feature of the church's mission which is derived from its largely Western origin. The burst of mission energy we know as the modern era of missions took its institutional form and owes a good deal of its success to organizational structures. What we know as agencies are independent corporate structures allowed to come into existence by Western law. Their genius is their goal orientation. Never mind the time-wasting question of whether these institutions are 'Christian' or not! The fact is that they permeate the missions scene, and the new surge of activity in the Two Thirds World is taking the same shape. They exist by the hundreds, and they are each at great pains to justify their existence by describing their own uniqueness. Each does this by distinguishing its goals or character ever so slightly from all others. The task may require of 'Give us your money and hands off!' In 2 Corinthians 8:13, 14 the Apostle talked about 'mutual supply'.

Allow me a simple illustration of the possibilities open to the Two Thirds World agencies. Catalogues of countries hostile to the gospel, and maps drawn to indicate restricted entry, are almost invariably (with a few delightful exceptions) based on governmental attitudes to Western missionaries. It is true that the laws sometimes exclude all 'Christian' missionaries, and some countries are quite closed. However, none are hermetically sealed, and in some cases Two Thirds World missionaries would find a warm welcome.

WHAT THEN IS NEEDED?

What is not needed is any grand advance in theory or theology. I do not want to disillusion anyone, but I do not believe that any sudden mind-blowing revelation lies around any corner we might soon turn. Nor is such a burst of light needed.

What we do need, it seems to me, are some simple practical steps to put in place the lessons we have already learned. They are as follows:

The agencies need to take specific unreached people groups as the definite focus of planning. Limited research, adequate to identify and describe the needs of these groups, is needed.

After this, it will be necessary to become familiar enough with the groups life to imagine what the church might look like as it develops. This picture will change with the passage of time. But forming it will remind us that we are not simply transferring our own cultural forms, and will provide the basis for setting goals to keep ourselves accountable.

We need strategies of ministry rooted in the needs of the groups. There is nothing mysterious about matching, in partnership, the resources God has brought together in the Church to minister to the full range of human need in Jesus' name. But we do need to think in terms of the whole Church as present or potentially present. This may require making some innovations and setting aside petty jealousies.

We need concrete goals, stated in a way that will allow us to tell if and when they are accomplished.

In short, we need to take the unreached peoples concept and purposefully, singlemindedly, set ourselves to identify, plan, join hands and minister.

(c) The growth of emerging missions, and their diversity:
    those concerned with *their own communities*;
    those concerned with *people who speak a similar language* in other countries;
    those concerned with working primarily *within their own countries*;
    those that are developing *an international nature*.

Future developments are uncertain, because differing priorities are being advocated. For some a moratorium is important. For others the accountability of Western agencies to the national churches is of the highest order. Still others argue that the priority of our age is the evangelization of the world and therefore para-church agencies have a right to proliferate in the fulfilment of this calling.

Given all this, it is imperative that the Church of Jesus Christ today not only define more closely its missionary calling and the nature of the need confronting it, but also the way in which it will undertake the task. With the growth of international mission structures today and the spawning of numerous mission agencies, as well as the continuous growth of churches in many parts of the world, it is imperative that urgent consideration be given to the issues of cooperation and coordination.

'The earth is the Lord's and the fulness thereof.' Therefore a duty is laid upon Christians to ensure that their God-given resources, in terms both of spiritual and material assets, are used to their maximum potential. The wastage which accompanies duplication of effort, and often conflicts of interest, does not glorify the Lord.

The escalating global population indicates the immensity and urgency of the church's mission to the evangelization of the world. But are the present mission structures capable of 'A church for every people by the year 2000', the clarion call of Edinburgh '80?

An important stepping-stone in the task of world evangelization is the establishment of indigenous mission agencies, because of:

(a) the enormous potential of the often-vibrant Christians outside the Western world in cross-cultural evanglism;
(b) the uncertain future politico-economic structure of the world.

Two-Thirds world missionaries can be trained in their own situations. Consideration should be given therefore as to whether these centres should exist in non-institutional forms. A closer examination needs to be made of the way in which Jesus Christ taught his disciples to be missionaries as opposed to the Western academic models of training. More coordination is needed between missionary institutions in order to facilitate greater interaction and to determine how and where help is needed. Resources will be needed both in terms of people and finance to assist such training centres to come into being, particularly in non-Western countries. The writing and publication of theological textbooks in many languages will be necessary for such local contextualized training.

(d) Cooperation needs to be fostered:
Between emerging missions and Western missions. Realistic and relevant patterns of cooperation must be developed. Greater thought should be given to the nature of partnership and whether this can culminate in integration.

Between Western missions and national churches. Urgent consideration must be given to the issue of accountability (the greatest issue facing missions over the next decade will be ecclesiology – what is the nature of the Church?).

Between Western agencies. The spirit of competition that all too often exists must cease and be replaced by more cooperation and greater respect for what others are doing.

Western agencies should not set up branches unilaterally in the Two Thirds World and then compete for the hire of the best national Christian leaders. Ideally the national Church should invite the agency to minister and the two should relate on that level. All too often:

> leadership is drained from the Church in these lands;
> the gospel is associated with Western leadership;
> the formation of models with which the nationals can identify is not made possible. There needs to be a sense of 'belonging', therefore an identity is needed.

(e) Resources must be used responsibly. Some key issues are:
Export of funds. Western missions should cooperate with emerging missions in countries where the transfer of funds is

(h) A theological conference should be convened to consider the shape of missions to come. It should take into consideration present trends in mission and the Church; theology; Biblical prophecy and secular forecasting (demographic trends, politics, economics, etc.).

demonstrate his rule over our lives for the good of the world.

1:4 The Church, throughout history, has been stirred up, guided and enabled by the Lord for its mission. Missionary societies, focusing on witnessing for Christ among groups distant from the Church, have made and are making a significant contribution to the worldwide expansion of the Church. It is a privilege to be co-workers together with Christ and we celebrate the growth of the Church in our own days. This is the Lord's doing and it is marvellous in our eyes. Nevertheless we recognise the immensity of mankind's continuing need, confess that our own sinfulness has contributed in part towards this, and pray that the Lord would continue to guide and enable his Church to fulfil the commission of its Lord and Master.

II. THE MISSION OF CHRIST

2:1 Mankind, created in the likeness of God, has fallen. His inner turmoil, selfish conflicts with his neighbour and abuse of the created earth all bear eloquent testimony to his alienation from God. Man does not have the capacity within himself to return to fellowship with his Creator, nor to true community with his fellow human beings. Yet his yearnings for reunion with God and for wholeness are felt in the writings and rituals of all religions and the attempts of men to pursue truth, justice and love. Historically the truth of God was maintained by holy men within the people of Israel, who, inspired by the Holy Spirit, foretold a coming Saviour of the world, who would suffer for the sins of mankind and would rise to bring mankind victory over death.

2:2 In the fulness of time Jesus of Nazareth came and fulfilled these prophecies as well as the longings and yearnings of mankind, and having made a way for man to be saved by his sacrificial death on the cross and his resurrection from death by the power of the Holy Spirit, the Lord ascended into heaven to sit at the right hand of his Father. His own teaching and that of his contemporary followers reveals that he is the only way to God and that apart from faith in him, man continues in his alienation and lostness, and is under the righteous judgment of God for his sins.

2:3 The full width and integrated nature of the Good News of for those who have never heard the Good News of salvation. There are still many groups 'without God and without hope in this world' (Eph. 2:12) who are beyond the easy reach of the existing churches. The Church is called to make disciples of all nations, not neglecting the more difficult ones, in order to fulfil its mission of evangelism to the world.

2:9 The compassion of Christ will additionally lead the Church to respond to human need in its many manifestations: individual and communal; economic, social, medical, political, educational. The teaching of the Church should encourage Christians to show justice and mercy. Rich Christians will simplify their lifestyles, open their homes and hear the cry of the oppressed in order to show justice to the poor. The Church needs to develop methods of prophetic address to those outside the church in order to rebuke evil and promote justice.

2:10 The Church needs to recognise those within her with special gifts for evangelism and church planting, as well as for social action. Some of her best men, her leaders, should be set aside for the task of planting churches cross-culturally. At other times churches may commission teams for evangelism or social action. All such workers who are sent out by the Church should be supported in prayer and financially. The teaching programme of the Church should train all of its members, as Jesus did the Twelve, for their part in the mission of Christ.

2:11 The world's population is growing at a tremendous pace. Despite the expansion of the Church in recent decades, it remains a fact the world's population who do not yet believe in the Lord Jesus also continues to grow. The Church needs to respond with compassion to this situation and to evangelize and plant churches among the many groups presently unreached by the gospel.

III. THE CHURCH'S RELATIONSHIP WITH MISSIONARY SOCIETIES

The nature of the Church

3:1 The Church is the total body of all believing men and women, past, present and future. Located in history, it grows and develops structure is unnecessary. New missions have liberty to create new structures for their new wine, according to need and their business and managerial traditions. This flexibility and variety should be encouraged and may renew the structures of older missions.

New models for mission

3:5 The worldwide moving of God's Spirit has seen multitudes ushered into the Kingdom, the creation of numerous churches and the launching of thousands of missionaries from these churches in the Two Thirds World. God's Spirit is challenging not only the form of our present mission structures, but also the way in which we engage in mission. Present forms need to be reassessed as to their relevance to today's world. Current practices of missions need to be reconsidered in the light of newly formed churches.

3:6 Many Western missions have opted for the internationalization of their structures, permitting them to recruit missionaries from many countries in the world. The rise in the number of newly-created Two Thirds World missions also is a cause for rejoicing. Some Western missions are exploring ways of entering into a mutually-helpful relationship with one or more of the Two Thirds World missions. Missions need to consider how to relate to other fellow-workers in the Great Commission.

3:7 There are a number of models of such cooperation already working to the positive benefit of both partners. These should be made known more widely and further experiments of cooperation should be encouraged: whether in the field of training, or in the sharing of personnel, finance, expertise or information. The new missions must have the freedom to make their own mistakes. Yet many of the problems which they confront have already been faced by older missions, whose experience should be made freely available.

3:8 The worldwide expansion of some rich Western-based organizations has caused anxiety in some Two Thirds World nations. This has been partly due to their hiring the best of the local Christian leadership, thereby stifling the development of local structures; partly because they tend to present one solution to the problems of the people of that area, based on a Western theology,

IV. THE MISSION OF THE CHURCH IN FRONTIERS OF HUMANITY

4:1 Having now seen the nature of the Church and missionary fellowships and that of the mission itself, we turn to those to whom the mission is directed. After the Creation, God blessed Adam and Eve and instructed them to 'be fruitful and increase in number' (Gen. 1:28). In Genesis 10, from the Table of Nations, it is evident that mankind although one in Adam is differentiated into a glorious variety of units. This variety within the unity of mankind continues to the present day and it will continue until the New Creation, in which, the book of Revelation shows, there will be worship of the Lamb from every one of these groups, 'a great multitude that no one could count, from every nation *(ethnos)*, tribe *(phule)*, people *(laos)* and language *(glossa)*' (Rev. 7:9). These varieties among the groups of mankind are not inherently evil but rather God-given. The relationships between these groups have often reflected the sinful nature of man – oppression, racism, war etc. – but the Good News of Peace through Jesus Christ (Eph 2:14) breaks down the sinful barriers between groups without harming their cultural identity. The Gospel does not have a culture. 'Christianity is always a beggar seeking for food and drink, cover and shelter from the cultures and times it encounters in its never-ending journey and wanderings' (John Mbiti). The gospel, then, is a way beyond cultural, political or economic imperialism.

4:2 The church at Antioch provides an example of a community of God's people, themselves drawn from a variety of groups, with an ethnically integrated leadership, and with a concern to witness across cultural and geographical barriers. It was a church through which such barriers were being broken down through the Gospel of Christ.

4:3 Mission to all the peoples of earth has been God's purpose from the dawn of redemptive history. The call of Abraham ends with the utmost incredible promise 'that all the peoples of earth will be blessed through you' (Gen. 12:3). This theme continues throughout the Old Testament and is seen most clearly in the Servant Songs of Isaiah. There God not only reveals the depth of Messiah's mission – his vicarious suffering and death – but the scope of his activity throughout history: 'I will also make you a light to the nations that you may bring my salvation to the ends

Jesus Christ – in many cases the way of doing this will be unique and will respond to the needs of the hearers.

V. THE MISSION OF THE CHURCH IN THE PROVISION OF RESOURCES FOR FRONTIERS

5:1 God, who made the world, has provided us in his Word with adequate guidance about how to use his world's resources. Mankind has often failed to heed this guidance and at this historic moment faces immense crises over his stewardship of the world's diminishing material resources.

5:2 Christ's teaching and his example of use of resources carries immediate significance for those who are engaged in the mission which he entrusted to the Church. The same Lord who directs this mission has said, 'All authority in heaven and on earth has been given to me, therefore go . . .' Our ascended Lord provides all necessary resources to his church for this task. The resources within the church are not the property of the Church but rather of him who purchased the Church with his own blood. We are his stewards, responsible to use these resources as he directs. It is necessary to establish a theology of resources in order to combat the present tendency for diverse priorities, pressure and ideologies to guide our decision-making in this area.

5:3 A study of the Acts of the Apostles reveals the primary importance of the spiritual resources which Christ grants to his church. The Holy Spirit, 'the absolutely indispensible resource of the Christian Church' (Dr Philip Teng), is the power through whom Christians are impelled and enabled to witness for their Lord. These early Christians were deeply devoted to the Apostles' teaching, fellowship, the breaking of bread and prayer. Historically, it has been noted that a spiritual dynamic, normally arising out of a renewal movement and based on fresh biblical insights, is an essential factor in every new missionary thrust.

5:4 The Incarnation of Christ and his subsequent training of the Twelve demonstrates that God entrusts human beings, members of the Body of Christ, with the responsibility of being his witnesses. In our words and actions we are to show Christ to the world for which he died, in hope that others will turn and follow Christ too.

the new missions are restricted by their government's law from exporting funds to their missionaries abroad. New models of co-operation must urgently be created which will enable the missionaries to be paid by another mission or third party.

5:9 We thank God for much of the recent scientific advance which has been of tremendous help to mankind in such fields as medicine and communications. The church, no less than the rest of society, needs to ask critical questions and to establish ethical guidelines about her use of such knowledge and equipment in the service of Christ. Such advances are already helping the Church in her diverse ministries. Radio offers great opportunities for presenting the message of Christ in locations where it is difficult to maintain a Christian presence; although the fundamental limitation of evangelism through mass media is that it can never be an incarnational witness.

5:10 There has been very large expansion in the Church's resources relating to information about mission. Some coordination is needed in order to avoid unnecessary duplication of research and susequent competition. Certain political situations and alignments can provide the Church with opportunities or hindrance in her witness. It is evident that while mission for some nationalities is made difficult to some peoples due to political, linguistic or cultural distance, there are sometimes other parts of the Body of Christ who are in a better positon to witness to them. Pragmatic considerations are not to be the final arbiter in the Church's relationships with various Governments and political systems, but rather it must be guided by the ethics of the Kingdom of God. Information about political, cultural and ethno-linguistic situations needs to be made readily available worldwide, to allow missions to plan their activities and to allow the possibility of coordination in reaching specific groups.

5:11 The parable of the talents calls individuals, churches, or mission structures, to responsible management in their use of resources. There is a lack of responsible management when mission agencies refuse to work together, or maintain a spirit of competition. God's Spirit calls the church to the creative and cooperative use of the resources so freely given by our heavenly Father for his purpose in the world.

background of his audiences. In Athens he quotes Greek poets. The missionary needs to be able to understand the culture and world view of the people among whom he is witnessing, and how to present the gospel relevantly to them, while yet avoiding syncretism.

Paul drew around himself a team for support and corporate witness. The missionary needs to learn the mind of a servant to be able to work in a team, which is often drawn from a wide variety of backgrounds.

Paul was able to support himself. In some circumstances Christian training will have to include or be supplemented by vocational training.

6:5 There need to be major new initiatives to enable missionaries from the Two Thirds World to train for cross-cultural witness. An international medium of exchange of training models would be helpful. Training for witness should not be restricted to 'professional missionaries' but should embrace all of the members of the Body of Christ. There are lay members in churches who have great opportunities in the course of their work to witness to groups which at present do not have a church among them. There is a need to create new models of training for professional missionaries and lay people. There is a need for less institutional, less academic, more practical and cheaper forms of training in addition to the present college-type structures which continue to be helpful in training Christian leaders and theologians. In recent years great strides have been made in creating new ways of training in cultural sensitivity.

VII. THE UNFINISHED TASK

7:1 The Church faces a growing missionary task. The escalating world population coupled with an uncertain economic future challenges God's people in today's world to respond with the compassion of Christ.

7:2 We can see the hand of God in new things in our day – the huge growth of churches in the Two Thirds World, the renewal of churches in the West, new understanding in theology, to name just a few. These are signs that the God of history does not, and